PADMAVATI

Katha Classics

Our Recent Releases

Short Fiction
Katha Prize Stories 10
   Ed. Geeta Dharmarajan
   & Nandita Aggarwal
Hauntings: Bangla Ghost Stories
   Edited and Translated by
   Suchitra Samanta
Forsaking Paradise: Stories from
Ladakh, Edited and Translated by
   Ravina Aggarwal
Ayoni and Other Stories
   Edited and Translated by
   Alladi Uma & M Sridhar
Home and Away
   By Ramachandra Sharma
   Translated by Padma and
   Ramachandra Sharma
Vyasa and Vighneshwara
   By Anand
   Translated by Saji Mathew
Joginder Paul: Sleepwalkers
   Translated by Sunil Trivedi and
   Sukrita Paul Kumar

ALT (Approaches to Literatures in Translation)
Ismat: Her Life, Her Times
   Eds. Sukrita Paul Kumar &
   Sadique
Translating Partition: Stories, Essays,
Criticism
   Eds. Ravikant & Tarun K Saint
Vijay Tendulkar

Trailblazers
Paul Zacharia: Two Novellas
   Translated by Gita Krishnankutty
Ashokamitran: Water
   Translated by Lakshmi Holmström

Bhupen Khakhar: Selected Works
   Translated by Ganesh Devy,
   Naushil Mehta and Bina Srinivasan
Indira Goswami: Pages Stained with
   Blood, Translated by Pradip Acharya

Katha Novels
Singarevva and the Palace
   By Chandrasekhar Kambar
   Translated by Laxmi
   Chandrasekhar

YuvaKatha
Lukose's Church
Night of the Third Crescent
Bhiku's Diary
The Verdict
The Dragonfly
The Bell

BalKatha
The Carpenter's Apperentice
The Nose Doctor
Grinny the Green Dinosaur
Battling Boats

Forthcoming
Daar se Bichchudi
   By Krishna Sobti
   Translated by Smita Bharti
Ai Ladki
   By Krishna Sobti
   Translated by Shivnath
Surajmukhi Andhere Ke
   By Krishna Sobti
   Translated by Pamela Manasi
Koonan Grove
   by Thoppil Mohamed Meeran
   Translated by M Vijayalakshmi

PADMAVATI

A MADHAVIAH

TRANSLATED BY MEENAKSHI TYAGARAJAN

KATHA

First published by Katha in 2002

Copyright © Katha, 2002

Copyright © for the English translation
rests with KATHA.

KATHA
A-3 Sarvodaya Enclave
Sri Aurobindo Marg
New Delhi 110 017
Phone: 652 4350, 652 4511
Fax: 651 4373
E-mail: kathavilasam@katha.org
Internet address: http://www.katha.org

KATHA is a registered nonprofit society devoted to enhancing the pleasures of
reading. KATHA VILASAM is its story research and resource centre.

Cover and inside Illustrations: M Krishnan
Courtesy: Indumati Krishnan
Kolams: Mukta Venkatesh
Cover design: Geeta Dharmarajan

General Series Editor: Geeta Dharmarajan
In-house Editors: Gita Rajan, Shoma Choudhury
Assistant Editor: Anuradha Rajkumari

Typeset in 12 on 16pt Lapidary333BT by Sandeep Kumar
at Katha and Printed at Kisa Offset, New Delhi

ISBN 81-87649-28-3

2 4 6 8 10 9 7 5 3 1

A Madhaviah

16 August, 1872 – 22 October, 1925

Madhaviah's residence, "Perunkulam House," Edward Elliots Road, Madras, where he lived until his death.

The "cottage" which housed his own printing press next to Perunkulam House.

Madhaviah with his family

Sitting (from left to right): Krishnan, Meenakshi (Madhaviah's wife), Lakshmi, A Madhaviah, Narayanan.
Standing (from left to right): Muthulakshmi (Mukta), Visalakshi, Anantanarayanan, Meenambal (Amba), Saraswathi.

CONTENTS

Introduction

No history of Tamil literature in the twentieth century can ignore the contribution of Anantanarayana Madhaviah to its prose and fiction. His best-known Tamil work, *Padmavati Charithiram,* is presented here for the first time in English translation. He was a pioneer, not only of the Tamil novel, but also of Indian writing in English. A brief account of his life and work is relevant to the fuller appreciation of this book.

Born on August 16, 1872 in Perunkulam, which literally means big tank, a village in India's southernmost district of Tirunelveli, Madhaviah completed schooling in the district town. Following his elder brother he moved to Madras (now Chennai), where he joined the Christian College. He had acquired an unquenchable zeal for both Tamil and English early in life. Gifted with a strong sense of prosody, he delighted in reading all the Tamil and English works he could lay his hands on. He came under the moral and intellectual influence of Reverend William Miller, Principal of his college, the only real life character appearing in *Padmavati*. He was fired with ardour to remove the evils and superstitions which beset his Iyer brahmin sub caste as well as the larger southern society of many jatis and faiths.

After taking the BA degree with a high rank, he became a teacher in the same college for a time. Following custom, he was married at the age of fifteen. He had to earn a steady livelihood to support his growing family, though he would have preferred to be a full-time writer. He took a competitive examination to enter the Salt and Abkari department and topped the list. Then began his years of service as a Salt Inspector, with postings from fishing hamlet to small town along the coast of Koramangalam (Coromandel), with his family in tow. This was the time when Madras Presidency included Andhra. One of his postings was in Ganjam district, near Orissa. He learnt Telugu, but somehow never studied Sanskrit.

Madhaviah enjoyed being an outdoorsman by day for his job's sake and a scholar-writer by lamplight for his fulfilment. A good rider, he loved horses. Swimming was another pastime he relished, once even venturing far into the sea for a wager, which he won in the form of a silver Victoria rupee. He was a man of rare courage – both physical and moral – but, the obverse was that he could never resist a dare. Once, at Kutralam falls, a favourite haunt of his, he heard that three Englishmen had tried to cross the top of the falls, only to be swept down to their death. Thereupon he attempted the feat, precariously stepping along the slippery rocks, mindless of his wife standing far below with her heart in her mouth. In this novel he gives an ecstatic, lyrical description of the falls and the refreshing quality of their waters.

Madhaviah began contributing pieces to Tamil journals from his early twenties. His friend, C V Swaminathier, with whom he quarrelled later, started a Tamil literary magazine, *Viveka Chintamani* in 1892. Here our twenty year old author began a serial, "Savithri's Story." Though unfinished, it has priority over Rajam Iyer's *Kamalambal Charithiram* (1896), which is said to be the first modern novel in Tamil. Madhaviah's fictional debut was published as *Muthumeenakshi* in 1903. It is a remarkable, forward looking novella, told in the first person, about the ordeal of a child widow who later marries a cultured man she had known all her life.

His early initiation in the art and craft of fiction spurred him to write a Tamil novel of ampler proportions. This became *Padmavati Charithiram*. Part One was published in 1898, Part Two in the next year. A young scientist who read it wanted his pre-teens bride to read it too as a preparation for their life together. Girls who read the novel would read it aloud to their daughters years later. Madhaviah was tempted to write a sequel and began Part Three around 1924, but it was left incomplete at his death not long afterwards. It is not included in this English version, but a summary is given after Part Two.

From Madhaviah's fluent pen issued a series of poems, songs, essays, plays and stories in both Tamil and English. The fiction drew on his experiences and his environment, with a marked tendency to arouse the dormant public to an agenda of social reform. This is evident in *Padmavati Charithiram* and his autobiographical English novel, *Thillai Govindan* (1903), which had the distinction of later being published by Fisher Unwin in London (1916). The latter novel charmed British readers in India because, as Frederick Harrison said in its preface, it afforded insights into, "The inner life of the vast mass of our fellow-subjects," with a "Fascinating picture of the contrasts and confusions of Hindu antiquity suddenly plunged into the whirlpool of modern Europe."

Madhaviah's oeuvre included sixteen short and long works in Tamil and thirteen in English, comprising stories for children, stories with a reformist message, and a Tamil prose rendering of "Othello" as "Udayalan." Two other English novels of his deserve notice – *Satyananda* (1909), about a boy who converts to Christianity, grows up, marries, and sets up an orphanage, and *Clarinda* (1915), a historical novel about a remarkable woman who is saved from sati by an Englishman and becomes a Christian. *Clarinda* is testimony to his assiduous research in eighteenth century politics, imaginative flair, empathy with the heroine and romantic vision of a common ground between the East and West.

Among the Tamil novels, *Vijayamartandam* (1903) is noteworthy. It is a racy romance, interspersed with songs, about a Marawa chieftain and his love for a belle from a hillside village.

The Salt Inspector's wandering days ended with his posting to Madras, about 1920. He eventually rose to become Assistant Commissioner of Salt and Excise, but not before a supersession, which rankled. It was the heyday of the Raj. South India was more torpid than fervid in the freedom movement, but for a few Moderates and fewer Extremists like the fiery poet Subramanya Bharati, a fellow Tirunelvelian. Madhaviah was no less a patriot. He passionately wanted India to be free. Though severely cramped by service rules, he dared to print some of his Tamil songs on the motherland in a collection called *Manjari* (1914). But he did admire the British for two things – their literature and their efficient administration. His relations with the British seniors were uneasy, for they were hardly tolerant of his literary pursuits. But he had several British friends among educationists and Tamil-loving missionaries. One of them, Fr Francis Kingsbury, wrote an ode in Tamil eulogizing him when he died.

Madhaviah's intellectual energy was not bounded by writing alone. He collected a personal library of Tamil and English classics, which he read, marked and digested. Besides a diary, he had a thick bound commonplace book called Nota Bene, wherein he recorded any quote or curiosity he chanced upon, all numbered and indexed in his own hand. He was a true Victorian in his epistolary exertions, corresponding with Sarojini Naidu and V S Srinivasa Sastry among others. In a bunch of brittle letters he left, there is one from Mahatma Gandhi and one from Rudyard Kipling.

Madhaviah was a devoted family man. He had eight children, the first five girls, and then three boys. He taught his wife to read English and improve her Tamil, like Narayanan in *Padmavati*. He personally trained all his children in both his beloved languages. All grew to be scholars who could write well. Two had books to their credit – my father, M Anantanarayanan, the eldest of the sons, and M Krishnan, the last born, a pioneering naturalist, photographer, writer and artist. Madhaviah's nephew – his elder brother's son, P N Appuswamy – came very much under his influence and shone later as a respected Tamil scholar, science writer and translator.

When he was about fifty, Madhaviah took premature retirement to devote himself to Tamil and to social reform. He started the Author's Press in his own house and began editing his own literary magazine called *Panchamritham* in 1924. He was then in seemingly sound health and at the height of his powers. He had a wide readership and many friends in disparate circles, including musicians (for he loved music, like Narayanan in the novel) and craftsmen, but his candour and unorthodoxy upset many, especially brahmins.

He had been chosen as a member of the Madras University's Senate. On 22 October 1925, after a speech to a Senate meeting on the need to have Tamil as a compulsory subject in the BA curriculum, he sank back with a heart attack and died. He was only fifty three years old.

Madhaviah was deeply impressed by the Christian ethic of philanthropic service, but he deplored the conversion of Hindus for convenience. He was also critical of ritualized Hinduism. He detested the priestly avarice of brahmins, which fed on rank superstition and unexamined convention. These attitudes come through in *Padmavati* and his other fictions. As a rational humanist, he was drawn towards both Buddhism and Advaita Vedanta. The Bhagavad Gita also influenced his evolving credo, as the penultimate chapter of *Thillai Govindan* reveals.

It remains to consider the relevance of *Padmavati* a century on. There is growing interest among historians and sociologists in reconstructing the colonial period for a better understanding of socio-political change. This novel conveys an authentic period picture of brahmin life in the rural south and of student life in Madras. It captures glimpses of three strata – the rich landholder, the dependent widow, the indigent student. The author had woven in plenty of circumstantial details of daily life. Even the wedding budget and the reference to prices and incomes help us to imagine those times in sharp focus. Much has changed and some shameful customs are obsolete or mitigated by the modern mode, like the shaving of the widow's head, which the lovely Savithri has to endure for life. But much remains which is still a horrid bane – the gender bias of the patriarchal household, the discouragement of girls' education, arranging early marriages for girls, the shabby treatment of widows, the rich man's concubinage, the prevalence of ruinously expensive ritual observances. Dowry does not figure as an evil in this novel, though in other works the author denounces it with scorn.

Padmavati is neither a tract nor a manifesto, but an engaging story about the maturing personality of a spirited young girl born into the rigid confines of brahmin domesticity. The narrative current sucks in a cast of variegated characters – the high minded, sometimes errant, but self-correcting Narayanan, his mother – illiterate, widowed, but with an innate self-respect and self-esteem that values self-reliance and refuses to accept charity, even a loving brother's, his friend Gopalan, from whom he temporarily drifts apart due to the perverse machinations of Gopalan's younger brother, Sangu, a colourful villain, Savithri, Gopalan's elder sister, wise and mature beyond her years, idealized by Narayanan, and several others, vividly drawn, credible, true to life, individuated in psychology and behaviour. Narayanan slips from the lofty standard of his guru, Reverend Miller, and cruelly mistreats his wife out of Othello-like jealousy. This theme recurs in Madhaviah's fiction. The plot is developed with care and artistry. Scenes of marital discord in different homes are subsumed by a faith in the enduring marriage of true minds. A curious feature is that all the main characters, except Narayanan's mother, tormented by their problems, contemplate suicide at some point of their lives. If the modern reader is jarred by the authorial intrusions, coy asides and moralizing, let it be considered in context — Madhaviah was adapting the form and temper of the Victorian social novel to his own very different background and culture, with an avowedly didactic purpose of persuasion through entertainment, in the old Indian tradition of the storyteller's art.

Padmavati Charithiram is the beginning of a new genre — the novel of contemporary life and society in a Tamil prose of supple vitality, simplicity and lightness of touch. The author's preface explains why he chose a simple style and diction embellished by occasional flourishes, literary quotations, songs and fine writing. The novel was also intended to be read by women without formal education who were yet capable of self-improvement.

The realistic social novel came late to Tamil. Madhaviah had forerunners in Marathi and Bengali. In Telugu, K Veerasalingam Pantulu had blazed a trail. His *Rajasekhara Charitra* had appeared in 1880. His use of the form to propagate modern ideas on women's education must have influenced Madhaviah. But it was Madhaviah who broke the path for Tamil writers like Pudumaippittan, Kalki and the modern novelists by showing that the novel could be a powerful literary form in a society sluggish to accept new values in changing times.

Translating a classic like this into English is particularly difficult because of the author's distinctive style and rhythm, his use of proverbs, verses and songs to illuminate his narrative. This version by Meenakshi Tyagarajan, the daughter of Madhaviah's eldest daughter, keeps faith with the Tamil text, letting the storyline convey the flavour of the original.

Clearly, Madhaviah was a most unusual man, far ahead of his time as an enthusiast of social reform, particularly the education of girls. His fifty three years were packed with vital activity and literary enterprise in two languages, a rarity down to our own times, even for a full-time writer. His experiments with different genres like the short story, the play, the historical novel and the literary essay and poetry were a guide and stimulus to later writers in Tamil. Sadly enough, his books are hard to come by even in his beloved Tamil country, which he served so handsomely with his creative drive. This novel is one work of his to be republished several times and must serve as his main legacy to the development of modern Tamil prose and fiction. I hope that *Padmavati* will reach a widening readership from many language groups, not excluding Tamils, from India and other countries.

I have drawn mainly on a family memoir by my uncle, M Krishnan and two articles in *Kalaimagal* by P N Appuswamy in preparing this note.

April, 2002.   A Madhavan

Translator's Note

I was introduced to *Padmavati Charithiram* very early. My mother, the eldest of Madhaviah's eight children, followed her father's example and exposed her children to good literature by reading aloud from English and Tamil classics. *Padmavati* featured frequently in these readings. It continued as a firm favourite, re-read from time to time.

However, the idea of a translation occurred much later. What began as a tentative experiment soon became a fascinating challenge as I experienced, at a remote second hand, a faint echo of the joy that must have been the author's as he wrote life into his characters.

My object was to present the novel in readable English without taking undue liberties with the original. This proved a task beset with problems and pitfalls.

It was impossible to capture in English the qualities of Madhaviah's Tamil style, a unique blend of classical purity, clarity and verve. The clever play on words and puns were of course untranslatable as also some phrases, expressions and proverbs. The fluent flow of long, involved sentences had necessarily to be broken up with some rearrangement and condensation to avoid repetitive sequencing. Particularly difficult were the long, exuberant descriptive passages and in this I found some abridgement unavoidable. This is most marked in the lyrical description of Kutralam in chapter five of Part Two. The description of Savithri in chapter eight of Part One has also been slightly condensed.

Another source of difficulty was the poetic embellishment with quotations from classics as well as the author's own poetry. Many of these have been translated and where this was not found possible, the substance of the verse has been given. For the rest, I have tried to remain faithful to the letter, the form and the spirit of the original.

A rich and unexpected bonus came my way in the form of sketches of characters and situations in the book by my uncle, M Krishnan, Madhaviah's youngest son. They were done many years ago, sometime in the fifties and were not intended for publication as reproduction would not have been possible with the technology then available. Krishnan had drawn them for his own amusement and then cast them aside – but his wife, Indumati, retrieved and saved them. As this translation progressed, she undertook a strenuous search, found the drawings and gave them to me. I am deeply beholden to Indu.

This book would have remained a mere idea but for the help of a number of persons. My grateful thanks are due: to Mukta Venkatesh, Madhaviah's daughter and my aunt, for her warm encouragement and critical comments and suggestions for improvement of an earlier draft; my cousin Madhavan for reading through the draft, offering suggestions and contributing the Introduction; Dr Prema Nandakumar, for giving me the benefit of her scholarly insight; Nalini Chettur for her friendly interest and valuable advice through the publication stage; Saraswathi Sankaran for elucidation of some Tirunelveli expressions and customs; Shanthi Krishnan and Nirenjan Krishnan for their cheerful and efficient secretarial support and last but not the least, Katha in the person of Geeta Dharmarajan, for taking the risk of publishing the translation – by an unknown translator – of a nineteenth century novel and for all their editorial efforts.

Chennai, April 2002   Meenakshi Tyagarajan

Padmavati was originally published in Tamil in 1898 as *Padmavati Charithiram.*

At Katha, there has been a conscious attempt to avoid using Indian words as local colour but to use them frequently and unobtrusively as they actually *are* used by most of us. Thus we have deliberately chosen not to italicize Indian words since we believe these belong and should belong to the English language as spoken and used in different parts of India. A few words have been glossed and the meaning or relevant information provided in a footnote in the belief that this information would bring alive the context of the story. Some words have been explicated, in the text, the first time the word is used.

THE AUTHOR'S PREFACE
TO THE THIRD EDITION (1911)

The English word "novel" and the Sanskrit term "navinam" are both derived from the same root and have the same meaning. While originally the English word indicated "newness," it has, through usage, become synonymous with a special class of writing, the narrative tales of imagination. In this genre, Westerners group the tales in which unusual and startling events predominate as "romances" while those which truly reflect life and adhere closely to everyday experiences are classed as "novels."

The latter category, "novels," in the English language includes the historical novel, the social novel, the religious novel, the novel of life in the higher strata of society and those of life in the lower strata, novels based on psychological research, et cetera. Though this form of writing has been in vogue for about two hundred years, it is only in the last fifty years that it has developed and expanded. At present, thousands of works in this genre are published every year. Besides, novels by well-known writers published in thousands are sold out within in a matter of months of their release. This form of writing is not brushed aside as something frivolous but accepted by intellectuals, scholars and poets, many of whom have written such works and gained fame. Just as certain attributes are linked to the heroes of our legends and myths – such as Arundati for chastity, Harischandra for truth, Dharmaputra for patience and Durvasa Rishi for anger – and these are so deeply ingrained in the minds of our people as to become proverbial, the characters of some famous novels are used with familiarity by Westerners in their ordinary conversation as well as in scholarly writing. The bookstalls installed in railway stations in this country and in others for the benefit of passengers, for the most part stock and sell novels. This indicates the popularity of such works. Further, the best English novels are translated into European languages and Englishmen translate similar works in other languages into English.

There was nothing similar to the English novel in Tamil literature, which has very few works of prose. The prose narratives of some Puranic tales, both constitute novels. To the best of my knowledge, the only works that can even approach that category are *Premakala Vatheeiam* and *Prathapa Mudaliar Charithiram*. Of these, the former cannot truly qualify for various reasons. The latter belongs to the category of "romances" which Westerners find inadequate and do not favour much. Desirous of introducing the genre in Tamil, which many in the civilized West appreciate and find intellectually stimulating, I had begun a novel, *Savithri Charithiram* in the first issue of the Tamil Magazine *Viveka Chintamani*. For some reason, it was not completed. Later, it was understood that the late Sri Rajam Iyer's *Kamalambal Charithiram* was published and then came *Padmavati Charithiram – Part One*. Following this, several novels came out, one after the other, so that now there are many novelists and several novels are published every year.

As with all good writings, the novel also seeks to please the reader while at the same time conveying good advice. It is not appropriate to examine here the essential qualities of a novel or to examine, in that light, Tamil novels that have appeared so far. But since the "novel" is truly "novel" in the Tamil language, one point is worth making. In the course of a narrative, it may be usual to employ colloquial, ungrammatical language while recording the conversation of some characters; but it is necessary that the author's own direct address should be pure and flawless. Since this genre is intended to benefit even those without much education, the adoption of as simple a style as possible is advisable. But if in this, grammar is sacrificed, it would earn the displeasure of the educated readers. And since those without much education – primarily women who are the main readers of these works – will not know the requirements of good language and are likely to be easily misled, it would be appropriate to adopt a proper literary style.

A Madhaviah

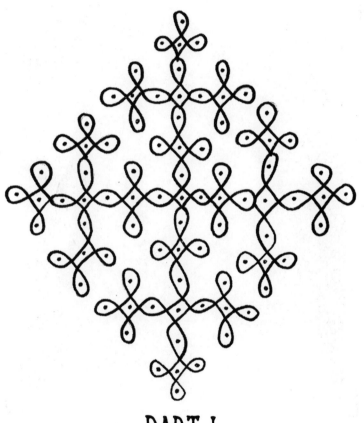

PART I

We ambled along, Manu singing some Dikshitar kritis. We had a delightful time but ...

Chirukulam was a small village in the Tirunelveli district of Pandyanadu in south Tamil Nadu. Of the two hundred odd houses in the village, all but the sixty occupied by the lower castes were brahmin households. As was usual in a small village, the two streets in which the brahmins lived were separate from the rest. There were no shops of any kind in the village, only backyards or, as the people there said, No kadais, only purakadais. Even for such basic condiments as pepper and ginger and daily necessities like betel leaves, tobacco and areca nuts, one had to go to Irangal, the port town, a full mile away.

Sitapathi Iyer, a brahmin of Chirukulam, possessed a tiny bit of land. While this was his main source of income, he sought to supplement it through other, not entirely honourable, means and somehow eked out a living. He was highly skilled in giving or preparing false witnesses, fomenting quarrels, creating trouble for the innocent through anonymous petitions and extorting money from the poor. The reputation he had earned roused fear not only in the minds of villagers ignorant of law but even among government servants, many of whom had suffered transfers, demotions, enquiries and humiliation because of his activities. Sitapathi Iyer proudly claimed that he had been instrumental in the transfer of as high an official as a Deputy Collector. He boasted that neither drought nor bountiful harvest made any difference to him as long as he had his Pen.

On a certain moonlit night, Sitapathi Iyer was relaxing on a coir cot outside his house, chewing his after dinner betel and chatting with Krishna Iyer and Rama Pillai. Their idle talk turned to the qualities of moonlight. Krishna Iyer agreed with Sitapathi that the full moon in the month of Maasi was without doubt breathtaking but he had misgivings about its nature.

"It is certainly not good for one's health," he said. "You know, last year, on such a night, indeed the moon was even brighter, I was returning from Irangal with West Street Nanu. We had eaten at Sivarama Iyer's place after attending his mother's vratha samapthi puja. We ambled along, Nanu singing some Dikshitar kritis. We had a delightful time but the cold and fever that followed had me sick for over a week. The usual native concoctions had no effect and I finally had to consult that apothecary, the one Sambu Iyer calls Apavatha Hari, in Irangal. Only *his* medication worked. Do pass me some betel leaves. And why don't you let me try that snuff from Kuppan Pillai's shop?"

Rama Pillai was skeptical. "Saami, all this talk of Maasi moon perpetrated by some worthless fellows is nonsense. If this moonlight is all that harmful, how is it that Nanu, who accompanied you, was not affected?" He went on to recite the old jingle about the need to beware of some particularly deceptive conditions – the moon in the month of Maasi, the portals of the disrespectful, a prostitute's favours and a merchant's friendship.

"Why include the merchant's friendship?" mused Sitapathi Iyer.

Krishna Iyer immediately elaborated, "Because it's apt. Take Meyya Rowther of Irangal, who claimed he was floating a company and looking for partners. One fine day he ran away to Mecca or somewhere with something like ten thousand rupees. May he be ruined! I'm ashamed to admit this in public, but I too lost fifty rupees. This is what a merchant's friendship means."

Narayanan, Sitapathi Iyer's young son, who until now had been listening silently to the conversation from his bed on the thinnai joined the elders and said, "No Appa, you can't generalize like this! Do you know that the whites ruling us now belong to the mercantile community? It is said there are some among them richer than mighty emperors. They can bring a war to a grinding halt by refusing credit to the warring factions. Can you categorize all of them as rogues? Are they not ruling us with justice?"

"Impeccable justice!" cut in Krishna Iyer, "No doubt they are all Dharmaputras, no less! Why, only yesterday I had to borrow thirty rupees for greasing the palm of an overseer in the engineer's office. Justice indeed!"

"But that is our fault!" cried Narayanan. "You can't blame the rulers for that! They give us jobs with a decent pay but we are dishonest. They do punish those whose misdeeds come out in the open. You can't condemn merchants and commerce as a whole for our dishonesty."

Rama Pillai, silent till then, quipped. "Why all this, saami? As the proverb goes, Speak during the day only after looking all around and at night avoid even that. I ask you, why seek such farfetched examples and blame only merchants? Aren't there amongst us innumerable cheats, liars and turncoats? There are even brahmins, sporting the sacred thread, who have no scruples about lying, killing or cheating. These crimes are their principal business and their commerce is indeed very specialized." Though he feared the lash of Sitapathi Iyer's tongue Rama Pillai warmed to his theme and looked directly at Iyer, thinking of the troubles and losses he had faced some years ago because of Iyer's activities.

Reaction was immediate. Sitapathi Iyer sprang to his feet. "You, you, vellala payale!" he screamed, betel juice from his mouth showering down on Krishna Iyer's head and face. "How dare you! You payale, come on say that once more and I'll cut off your tongue!"

The outburst scared Rama Pillai but did not silence him. "Mind your language, saami! What do you mean calling me payale? Did I take any names? Ask Krishna Iyer here, did I? Well, it seems like the pumpkin thief dusting his shoulder ..."

Reason and common sense desert an angry person. Sitapathi Iyer was always easy to provoke and when roused, the little common sense he possessed deserted him. Before Rama Pillai could finish, he shouted, "Ennada payale, you call me a pumpkin thief?" and slapped Rama Pillai sharply on the face. Pillai retaliated. The din brought out the neighbours, some of whom took up Sitapathi Iyer's cause, either out of fraternal feelings (Rama Pillai, belonging to the vellala caste, was after all the outsider in this brahmin neighbourhood) or fear of Sitapathi Iyer. Rama Pillai was badly battered and suffered serious injuries. Bleeding from his wounds and shouting profanities he went home, collected some men of his own caste and staggered straightaway to the house of the Sub Magistrate at Irangal. Meanwhile Sitapathi Iyer, calmed down by his neighbours, went to bed blissfully ignorant of Pillai's trip to Irangal. But his wife could not sleep a wink that night.

All that his wife was left with as testimony of her marriage was her taali.

Narasimha Mudaliar, the Sub Magistrate of Irangal, was a ruthless administrator. Popular belief was that it was his severity that kept the bad elements around town in check. By virtue of his long service in the town, he had gained inside information about the troublemakers and wastrels in the entire area under his jurisdiction. Generally speaking, the lure of lucre did not entice him to deviate from duty. According to some gossips, he had, in his previous posting at Chendur, accepted a bribe of five thousand rupees in the Alwarayan murder case, and it was this suspicion that had caused his transfer. But according to him, he had secured his transfer only by pleading with the Collector. This explanation had to be accepted since an official of his standing surely could not be suspected of lying. However, some said that even after assuming office in Irangal he continued to receive, under pressure from well wishers, not hard cash but various gifts in kind – a bullock cart, a few heads of milch cattle, silk garments and the like. Can you ever hush up gossip? The jealous are always likely to say what they like. We should not accept all that as vedavakyam or the absolute truth, but be discerning about the veracity of the reports. Generally speaking, Narasimha Mudaliar, unlike some other Sub Magistrates, did not succumb to the temptations of the supply of daily necessities like rice, bananas and firewood. It has to be admitted that he was, on the whole, as honest as possible. However, he did have one great weakness, which he never bothered to conceal. This was his unbridled interest in the fair sex.

Whether this can be considered serious enough is debatable. Our mythology is replete with tales of gods succumbing to the love of women. Does not the *Meingnana Vilakkam,* the seventeenth century text on vedantic philosophy and puranic tales, speak of the power of Manmatha's arrows?

> *Brahma blanched,*
> *Vishnu turned red,*
> *And Siva, dark from top to toe.*
> *Manmatha, he with the thousand eyes,*
> *Wielder of the invincible weapons, says,*
> *Is there one who can withstand my arrows?*

How can man, a mere mortal, be superior to the immortals? It has been said that lust is as much an inherent part of man's nature, as fragrance in a flower, oil in a sesame seed and chime in a bell. It is born with man and will die only when his life departs. In the case of Narasimha Mudaliar, just as his authority over others and his superiority were established facts, his interest in this respect was also marked, evident even in ordinary conversation.

Narasimha Mudaliar had had an eye on Sitapathi Iyer for long. Sitapathi had once appeared as an accused before him. While lack of evidence had necessitated acquittal, he had not forgotten Sitapathi and was awaiting the next chance, like the hungry stork patiently awaiting the choicest fish, letting the small fry swim past. Besides, there was Rama Pillai's mistress, a lovely woman who never disobeyed Pillai.

Sitapathi Iyer's case was taken up for hearing on the ninth of Panguni. Rama Pillai had engaged Vakil Thiruvadia Pillai, to present his case with clarity, while for the defence there were two vakils, Swaminatha Iyer and Maddon Dorai.

The second witness for the prosecution was none other than Narayanan, son of Sitapathi Iyer. Taking oath in the witness box he said, all in a rush, "My name is Narayanan. There ... over there ... that is my father, I am his son." This caused titters in the court but Narayanan continued, "I am from Chirukulam, I am fourteen years old, I am a school boy."

This evoked a stern response from the Magistrate. "Stand up straight, Iyer! Don't droop like a girl who has come of age. Surely you can't stand like this when your wife joins you one day! Who told you to tell all this?"

Narayanan said, "Vakil Swaminatha Iyer."

"Oh, I see! Iyer has tutored you! Very well. What do you know about this case?"

"My father was not in town on the day of the fight. He had gone to Kurumpottraiyur to buy cattle."

"Very well. You say your father was not in town on the day of the fight. Now who fought whom? Speak up. Don't be scared. Don't bow your head like a new bride. Look at me and speak."

Narayanan stammered, "The fight, between Rama Pillai and ... Rama Pillai ... and ... and ... I don't know. Vakil Swaminatha Iyer will be able to say."

This was greeted with resounding laughter in the court. Narayanan had read somewhere that a veritable web of deceit could result from a single lie uttered to cover up a wrong. His mother Seethai Ammal, who abhorred her husband's crafty ways, took special care to inculcate honesty and uprightness in her son. Even as a child, Narayanan knew that a denial of stealing sweets incurred his mother's wrath, whereas confession brought him not punishment but rewards, more sweets and a loving kiss. Besides, his teacher Rajagopala Iyer took great pains to develop virtues in his students. In this matter of lying to save his father, Narayanan had needed great persuasion, both from his mother and his teacher. It is possible to bend a sapling in a desired direction. But a full grown tree cannot be made to change direction. Though reluctant, Narayanan ultimately agreed, seeking to assuage his conscience by shifting the onus of the lie to the vakil who had tutored him. He did not realize the great harm that would follow.

"I see!" the Magistrate said, "Well, Iyer, what did you say your name was? Narayana Iyer? Very good. Now just tell me one thing truthfully. You seem to be honest, unlike other brahmin fellows. Just tell me, did Rama Pillai hit your father first or was it your father who first raised his hand?"

Narayanan, eyes brimming with tears, said, "Rama Pillai used abusive language first."

"Yes, that is true," said the Magistrate, "Rama Pillai spoke first, I know. He after all, is a rascal. But whose was the first blow?"

Narayanan repeated, "Rama Pillai started shouting. So my father hit him and he retaliated. That was how the fight started."

Narayanan was asked a few more questions about the other accused and that was the end of his deposition. The vakils were spared the trouble as their job had been done by Narasimha Mudaliar himself. Though the defence lawyer, Maddon, objected, it was of no use. The deposition of one other witness may, however, be of interest.

That was a witness for the prosecution, Panchangam Pappu Sastri. He was wearing a dirty veshti of twelve cubits mended in twenty four places, and yet with about thirty holes, in the panchakachham style. A similar upper garment, the angavastram, resembling the rope used for churning butter, was twisted around his waist. When his name was called, he lifted his veshti and tucked it up to his thigh as a mark of respect for the court. He was keen on pleasing everyone and displayed in a wide grin each of his uneven teeth as he looked round the court greeting one and all, offering namaskarams and aasirvadams. The way he saluted the European lawyer, striking his forehead as if bemoaning his fate, brought forth laughter from all, including the accused.

The Magistrate said, "Oi Sastriare! What do you know?"

Pappu Sastri said, "I have studied ganantham, also some poetry and grammar. I have acquired proficiency in tarka sastra as well. Further, I know by heart all the kriya mantras of all castes and varnas backwards to forwards."

The entire court laughed at this.

The Magistrate said curtly, "Sastriare, stop this! I know about your accomplishments. So does the whole town." There was more laughter. "That was not what you were asked. What do you know about the case?"

"Your Honour should not be angry with poor me. I am a brahmin. Even Sri Krishna Bhagawan has said, Brahmana mama devata. One should honour brahmins. It will not be in Your Honour's interest to insult me."

This angered the Magistrate. "Don't you understand, you pappan, that you were told to shut up? I asked you to stop your nonsense and give a straight answer. Be careful. Did you think this is a house where a tithi is to be performed?"

"Oh no, I'll obey you. I know nothing about this case."

Thiruvadia Pillai, the prosecuting lawyer, asked, "What iyervaal, were you not present when the fight took place?"

"Vakil pillaivaal, you have to consider my position. I am a common man. Sitapathi Iyer is my friend. So is Rama Pillai. Did I not request right at the start that I should not be called as a witness? Do I poke my right eye or my left?"

The Magistrate cut in, using the derogatory form of addressing a brahmin, "Oi Pappan! Pay attention to what you say. If you tell a lie under oath, I can send you to prison. Be careful."

Sastri replied, "Fate rules everything. What is it that we can do?"

Thiruvadia Pillai asked, "How did the fight begin?"

"Sitapathi Iyer was talking in front of his house. Suddenly there was a lot of shouting. I was on the thinnai of the adjoining house."

"Who shouted first?"

"Both. I can't be specific."

The lawyer said, "Let that be. After all you were on the thinnai next door. You must have seen everything. Who struck the first blow?"

"I'm a common friend. Fearing this sort of a thing would follow, I cupped both my ears with my hands and shut my eyes tight. I know nothing of what happened thereafter."

This caused further laughter in the court.

The case went on for a week. At the end of it, the Magistrate sentenced Sitapathi Iyer to six months' rigorous imprisonment and fined him a hundred rupees, while Krishna Iyer and three other brahmins were fined fifty rupees each. With his lawyers' fees and police costs, Sitapathi Iyer's expenses totalled four hundred rupees. Another hundred was added by his futile appeal to a higher court which only confirmed the sentence. Once he was behind bars, many of his enemies took courage and came up with charges against him. A merchant filed a case for forgery of documents. As a result, the district court sentenced him to another four years of rigorous imprisonment running concurrently with his earlier prison term.

His fixed assets, a little land and a house, were liquidated as was his wife's jewellery except for her tirumangalyam.

All that his wife was left with as testimony of her marriage was her taali on a saffron thread. And Narayanan.

The boys then dispersed as noisily as honeybees from
a disturbed beehive.

C hirukulam had only one small Tamil school. Those wanting to learn English had to go to the Christian Missionary School at Irangal. Rajagopala Iyer was the senior teacher there. Though not possessing the academic distinction of advanced degrees, he had adequate knowledge of English besides deep learning in Tamil and a good grasp of Sanskrit. However, it was not his scholarship that distinguished him as much as his character. Unlike the general lot of teachers, he took great pride in his profession and did not consider it inferior to government service.

There can be no profession nobler than teaching, caring for the young even more than a mother would, shaping their minds and providing them with the right guidance. In all other professions there could be some scope for wrong doing – lying, cheating, exploitation and the like. But not in teaching which, like charity, blesses both the giver and the receiver. Man, endowed with base instincts from birth, escapes a bestial existence only through instruction – from his parents, friends, relatives and above all, his teacher. Can one thank a teacher adequately for this service of setting one free from a cattle-like existence governed only by hunger, thirst, sleep and lust? Alexander the Great, whose conquests spread over two continents, and whose fame reached the shores of the Ganga when he was barely thirty, was supposed to have said that he received life from his father Philip but it was his teacher Aristotle who was responsible for shaping that life. When once the question arose as to who the true lord of a land was, while many views were expressed, an elderly citizen emphatically stated that it was not the king, but the instructor who equipped the king, his ministers and executives with the skills necessary for governance.

What are the qualities needed in a teacher for him to discharge his important responsibilities? An effective teacher has to be endowed not only with intelligence and purity but with immense patience and a naturally sympathetic temperament. But not even one in a thousand of our village teachers possess these attributes. Many of them are perennially ill-tempered, snapping at their charges like rabid dogs. Some go a step further and take to beating their pupils, driving them like cattle. Many have only the most rudimentary knowledge of the subjects they are supposed to teach and resort to caning and pinching students as aids to teach whatever little they know. Men who have failed to learn anything of value take to teaching as a means of livelihood. We have even heard of a convicted thief, who emerging from a seven year prison term, and failing to secure any other means of livelihood, started a school! How can he, who never handled a pen, teach children? So many who have mastered nothing other than corrupt practices take on the task of moulding young minds. Many become vakils. Couldn't they have left it at that? Did they also have to become teachers? Why is it assumed as absolute truth that those who can do little else can teach? Until this outlook changes and some reform is brought about, our country cannot progress.

Both the morning and evening sessions at the Irangal school started with a brief prayer, consisting of the reading of a few sentences from the Bible. Some foolish parents refused to send their sons to this school, preferring an idle, homebound life steeped in ignorance for their children. But the majority, aware of Rajagopala Iyer's sterling qualities, had no reservations about enrolling their sons in a school in which he taught. He used to point out that the Sandhyavandhanam slokas state that just as the water raining from the skies falls at various places but ultimately flows into the ocean, prayer in any form or name, is ultimately accepted by Kesava, the god of gods. What was important was instilling an element of piety in the minds of the students, letting them know that good deeds would be rewarded and evil ones punished, and making them realize the truth that they were ultimately accountable to the Supreme Being for all actions. His argument was, Once they reached maturity they would understand the truth themselves.

The Irangal school had many small rooms, one for each class. In one of these, Rajagopala Iyer was seated at a table with about thirty boys sitting at desks, facing him. From the fact that he had closed the book on his table and the boys had packed their bags, it could be surmised that the day's lessons were over and the children were ready to return home. Our friend, second witness Narayanan, was in this class. He had just been called upon by the teacher to recite the kural taught the previous day. Narayanan's mind was elsewhere and he stood up and said, "It was Padmi who told me ..." at which the entire class burst into laughter. Narayanan, head downcast, eyes brimming, stood deeply shamed. "Idiot, keep standing!" the teacher muttered angrily and asked the next boy who promptly recited the Tamil couplet and explained its meaning as well – A learned man was honoured equally at home and elsewhere and only a foolish man chose to remain ignorant throughout his life. The teacher then asked if any one could remember any other verse with the same substance. Some students scratched their heads and some their elbows looking at each other. In the silence Narayanan, mustering courage, recited the verse – A king is honoured only in his own land while a savant commands respect wherever he goes.

Rajagopala Iyer was pleased. "Smart boy. That's exactly what I had in mind. See, you were inattentive and it caused you embarrassment. You must always concentrate on the job in hand. Some people think they can save time by tackling two or three jobs at a time, thereby spoiling all. There is an English proverb – One thing at a time and that done well. The poetess Auvaiyar also has a similar maxim, Whatever is attempted should be done correctly. Sit down. Don't be careless henceforth. All right boys, the bell has rung. You may leave." As he rose, Narayanan reminded him that he had not given them the kural to be memorized the next day. The teacher smiled, "See, I too have forgotten! For tomorrow it is not a kural but the verse ending with the words Karumame kannainar, about the concentration of those determined to achieve their goal, that has to be learnt along with its meaning." The boys then dispersed as noisily as honeybees from a disturbed beehive.

Seethai Ammal, muttering Sivasiva, Sivasiva, sat with streaming eyes.

Narayanan was, by nature, sensitive and shy. The embarrassing incident in class made him avoid his fellow students on the way back. As he entered Chirukulam's main street, a little girl peeping from one of the larger houses ran inside shouting, "Athai, Athai! Where are you? You were worried Appa would be late and there was no one to read the letter. But Nanu has come. He will read out all that I couldn't." She ran out to hug Narayanan's legs as he entered the house and dragging him by the hand, said, "There is some news Nanu, come in quick."

Seethai Ammal took one look at her son's face and asked, "Appa Nanu, what's wrong, child? Was something wrong with your tiffin? Are you hungry?"

Narayanan said, "It's nothing, Amma. Because of this kutti I was the laughing stock of the class today. I am a little upset by that."

A snivelling voice came from the kitchen, "Why should you suffer because of her? What can she do! Isn't it bad enough that I am born a woman and wedded to your uncle?"

Narayanan hastened to reply, "No, no, it was nothing much, really. It was entirely my fault. Padmi had recited an Ammanai song this morning when I was teaching her. I was thinking about it and when the teacher asked me a question, I replied absentmindedly, It was Padmi who told me, and everyone laughed." Even as he said this, the little girl, Padmavati, began to sing,

> Give me good sense,
> The sense not to fight and drive away,
> Those who seek my doorstep,
> Seek it in hunger, Ammanai.

Seethai Ammal said, "Is that all? Is this trifle bothering you? Let those who want to laugh, do so. Their mouths will ache. Look, here is a letter from your father, the first after so many days. I had to pay three pice to receive it. Padmi isn't able to make head or tail of it. She says it is in running hand. Do read it out."

The letter ran as follows,

Sivamayam

Tiruchirapalli Jail, Aavani 12th

To my brother-in-law Ayyavu. May he be blessed with wealth, all that he desires and a long life. I look forward to hearing about the well being of all of you. There is no point in telling you about my sufferings here. The only source of sustenance is keppai koozhu or kanji. I have to work every day like the untouchables in our village. There are men of all castes here and everyone has to live together. I have become so thin that you won't be able to recognize me ..."

At this point, Narayanan, overcome with sorrow, could not proceed and began to weep, while his mother sobbed loudly. Seeing them, Padmavati too began to cry. Her mother, without emerging from the kitchen, muttered, "What a fuss! Has there been a death in the house or what?" After a while, Narayanan composed himself and continued reading,

Brahma has destined that I, a brahmin by birth, have to do the work of menials. Any pause in the work, out of sheer exhaustion, brings on sharp blows. There is nothing to alleviate my lot – neither betel, nor tobacco, nor snuff. Ordinary mortals cannot understand the torture one undergoes if these habits are suddenly discontinued. Only

Narayanamoorthy, that Supreme Being, can understand my travails. No oil except what is used to make the keppai koozhu is available. So, there is no question of an oil bath. The sacred thread and tuft were lost long ago. I realize now that all this is the consequence of my misdeeds. What is the point in quarrelling with fate? One has to suffer the outcome of one's karma. You may recall Chuppu Pillai who earned a seven year sentence on my testimony for the theft in West Street Krishna Iyer's house. His glee on seeing me a prisoner knows no bounds. He has regained all the weight he had lost and is growing fat. I am so ashamed of my condition that I can hardly meet his eye. What can I say? I have been able to write this letter only because of the kind grace of a very compassionate gentleman, the Jail Writer, Sri Duraiswami Iyer. This honourable gentleman needs a good mat. Please get one of the best varieties from Pathamadai and send it to his address as soon as you can. I hope you will not let this matter slip your mind. I cannot even dream of my release. I may, at the most, live for a year more. You have to provide sanctuary to my wife and son. I know that you will take care of them always. Young Nanu is very intelligent. I had great hopes for him but god's will seems otherwise. He is dearer to you than to me. I cannot repay you for all this in this life but can only pray that Lord Subramanya shower his blessings on all of you and provide you with the best of everything.

With my blessings and seeking Lord Subramanya's grace,

Sitapathi Iyer,

Prisoner No 386, Main Jail, Tiruchirapalli.

While the letter was being read out, Seethai Ammal, muttering "Sivasiva, Sivasiva," sat with streaming eyes and hands on chin. After he finished reading, Narayanan lay face down and sobbed silently. Padmavati sat by his side, weeping. Seethai Ammal, to give vent to her feelings, moved to the backyard where she wept her heart out, lamenting the tribulations of her husband living on keppai koozhu, while she enjoyed delicacies. She wished death would claim her soon.

She found Narayanan lost in reverie looking at the ceiling,
an English book spread on his chest.

P admi, Padmi, don't play with that kutti, Seshi, you'll catch her eye infection. Go upstairs and ask Nanu to teach you. Go study," said Ayyavier, one evening. His wife, Subbammal, who was combing her hair, piped up, "Oh yes, indeed, do go and study! You have to appear for your BA exam soon! The District Collector's post is vacant and you are to be appointed. Please go. It's not necessary to learn household skills. Take care of your studies, that will do."

Her husband flared up. "Why are you barking, you dog? Does she have to learn any job from you? Isn't your own excellent work sufficient? How can any one else be appointed Collector while you're there? Shut up your big mouth and keep quiet."

"Why should I bark? I'm not a dog. I don't go picking at discarded dinner leaves. Nor do I go around begging for food," said Subbammal curling her lips scornfully and making a face.

Seethai Ammal, silent till then, joined in, "Yes, you're right, amma. I'm indeed a dog begging for food. I've had to leave my home, just there on the other street and come to your house. But I haven't come to any stranger's house, only to my brother's. After all, what you're enjoying now was saved by my father."

Enraged, Subbammal jumped up. "This is my husband's house and it belongs to me. Your father's claim ended with him. You've no right, do you hear? This is not your husband's house. It seems he's been given a large house in Tiruchirapalli. Why don't you go there?"

An infuriated Ayyavier sprang up and rushed at her, "What did you say, you cur, you donkey?" Catching hold of her hair he began raining blows and kicks on her. Subbammal howled that she was being killed. Seethai Ammal dropped her work, and ran up to release Subbammal's hair from her brother's clutch. "Ayya, please, please don't hit her," she pleaded. "Stop this. It's very wrong to harm a woman. It will have dire consequences. Let her say whatever she wants. It doesn't matter. Do we chop off a finger because it hurts our eye? Such anger isn't good for you." She was able to make him sit down for a while. Subbammal groaned loudly, "Adeyappa, Adiyamma, I'm dying, I'm dying." Ayyavier left the house in anger. Subbammal immediately sat up and poured her pent up fury on her sister-in-law.

"There has been nothing but misery in this house ever since you've come," she said. "What have I done to deserve all this? My parents should have tied a stone round my neck and pushed me down a well rather than marry me into this family. They were attracted by the property. Property indeed! What pleasure have I derived from it? My lot is to slog, slog for devils and dogs. Iswara, deivamé, don't you have any pity? Are you blind? When will I see dawn? You gracious sumangalis, if you accept me as the true wife that I am, gather me into your midst," she ranted and raved.

Seethai Ammal said, "Amma Subbu, don't torture yourself. Please forgive all the trouble I've caused you so far. I have never meant harm, either in deed or thought. Fate cruelly deprived me of everything. I could only seek support from my brother who, by god's grace, is fairly well off. And he too invited me to stay here. I thought, since I had no one else, I could stay here, living on kanji, at least until my grief subsided a little. I work in this house to the best of my ability. But this cannot go on. Even Chandramati and Lohidasan did not suffer at Kalakousikan's place like this. Your behaviour is intolerable. I can get this food anywhere, if nowhere else, there is the Malayala Maharaja's

---

Kalakousikan: The keeper of the cremation ground under whom Raja Harishchandra had to serve during his banishment by Sage Vishwamitra. **Ootuporai:** Charitable outlets serving free food were common in the Kerala kingdoms of old.

ootuporai. Or, my boy can seek alms at a few homes to meet our meagre needs. Don't worry, we will leave soon enough."

"Oh," said Subbammal, "You want to torture me further. You want to have the satisfaction of telling your brother that his wife is driving you out of the house. Only when I die will you be happy."

"Stop, don't say that. Why should you die? You who have so much to live for. May you live long and bear more children. What will I gain by your death? Let me learn of your happiness from afar. I'll give other reasons for going away. Rajagopala Iyer is leaving soon for a better job. Nanu has been saying that he'd like to change to some other school. We'll move to Tirunelveli."

"Great! You and your son will set up house in Tirunelveli and a money order will have to be despatched every month. Are you going to be bothered by my household's needs?"

"You don't have to worry on that score. As long as I'm able-bodied, I won't accept anything from you. You don't have to send me a copper coin," said Seethai Ammal.

Let us see what Padmavati, who went upstairs following her father's instructions, is doing. When she went up she found Narayanan lost in reverie, looking at the ceiling, an English book spread on his chest. He did not notice her coming in. Silent as a cat, she crept up stealthily and jumped from behind shouting "Duss." A somewhat startled Narayanan said, "Where have you been all this while, Padmi? You should have come for your lessons long ago." Padmi (we will refer to her thus for she is, after all, the heroine of our story and only a little girl besides) said, "I was out playing. But why are you looking at the roof? Are there any paintings there? Or perhaps you were wondering when you'd be getting married."

Narayanan smiled. "Nothing of that sort. I was thinking of father and the torture he's undergoing in prison. It depresses me so much that I sometimes feel I'll go mad," he said tearfully.

"Why was Athimber sent to prison? They said something then, I've forgotten."

"What could I do?" said Narayanan. "Everyone says he was sentenced because of my testimony. I was under oath and to the questions put to me in court, I couldn't help saying what was on my mind. But that sentence was only for four months and was over long ago. He now continues in jail for forgery. How can I help it?"

Padmi clung to his back, clasped his neck and with her cheek against his, rocked gently saying, "You won't do anything like that, will you?"

Before Narayanan could reply, they heard the sound of the fracas downstairs and Subbammal's wailing. Padmi merely said, "Maama and Ammami are quarrelling about something," and paid little attention to it, from which it can be concluded that such incidents were not unusual.

Padmi said, "Nanu, I've just thought of something. Won't I get a nice silk sari for your wedding?"

"Yes, indeed you will and you can wear it then. But for now let's finish some lessons."

"Tell me one more thing and then I'll study. Whom are you going to marry?"

"Marry? Why, the wall, perhaps. Amma and I have no means of livelihood. Appa has left us in such a state. But for Maama, we would've starved to death. Marriage is the last thing on my mind right now."

"Why do you worry? We've lots of food at home. Cartloads of paddy keep arriving. You can surely consider marriage. Why don't you marry me?"

Narayanan laughed and patted her back. "You? Why yes, indeed! I will. But only if you're not naughty and study well."

Padmi said eagerly, "Yes of course, I won't be naughty anymore! I'll even give up my puppy. And I promise to study well. But I'll marry only you. I feel so lonely until you come back from school. How can I live without seeing you? If I marry someone else, he might beat me as Maama beats Ammami. That's not right. I know for sure that you won't beat me. I'll marry only you."

Narayanan said, "I'll certainly beat you if you turn into a shrew like Ammami."

"Me? Oh never! Even if I do something wrong unknowingly you'll correct me, won't you?"

Narayanan felt this had gone far enough. "Don't be a silly girl," he said. "All this is fantasy. Your mother wants you to marry someone grand – a graduate, good looking and very rich. If such a bridegroom can't be found, she will get you married to Kittu, her athaan's son. Even if Maama were to agree, she would never, never allow it."

Padmi was adamant. "It won't be so. I'll marry you and only you. I'll never agree to marry Karikittu, that darkie. Now, promise you'll marry me. If not, I won't study and I'll pinch you hard." She proceeded to carry out her threat and Narayanan had to plead with her to stop. Padmi insisted on a promise and Narayanan finally said, "Yes, yes, I promise, now stop pinching. It hurts." After a moment's thought, Padmi said, "May I keep the puppy, please? Only that, I won't ask for anything more or be naughty."

Narayanan smiled, "All right, keep the puppy but don't twist its ears."

Lessons for the day started on this happy note.

He immediately wrote to Ayyavier requesting him to let
him know the real position.

His sister's decision to move to Tirunelveli was strongly opposed by Ayyavier. In the end, he agreed, with reluctance, considering Narayanan's education. Thereafter, he collected vessels and other household necessities as well as two to three months' provisions and loading them in his bullock cart, accompanied Seethai Ammal and Narayanan to Tirunelveli. His wife, totally opposed to such lavish gifts, raised no objection, consoling herself, Let the turban go, after all the head has been saved.

Ayyavier took all necessary steps to settle his sister and nephew at Sindhupoonthurai. After admitting Narayanan in the nearby Hindu College, fixing a house at a rent of one rupee per month and buying clothes, books and other necessities, he set out to return to his village to oversee the cultivation of his lands. He planned to send a monthly remittance but Seethai Ammal was adamant in her refusal. "Ambi," she said, "You are a samsari. You have a child and will have more. You should not take on the liability of another household. I need to work, how else can I pass the time? I intend taking in boarders, some of Nanu's schoolmates. In the first place, it is a useful job. So many children come here to study, leaving their parents and homes. Giving them wholesome, tasty, home cooked food is a fulfilling service. It's nothing to be ashamed of, not as if I'll be running a club where all and sundry come to eat. Nanu and I are greatly indebted to you. The rice we eat is yours. Nanu has come thus far only because of you and he still has a long way to go. We've no one other than you in this world. Please don't misunderstand me."

She spoke with feeling and did not relent, despite her brother's insistence. Finally, she softened slightly agreeing to write to him when short of money. Ayyavier left, asking them to write once a week without fail.

Some days later Narayanan received an envelope. On opening it he found two letters, one from his uncle and the other pasted over with a large lump of cooked rice. Ayyavier's letter read thus,

Chirukulam, Karthigai 13th

Aasirvadams to my nephew Nanu. May he be showered with all blessings. By god's grace, all are well here. I received your card. Do keep writing often to inform me of your wellbeing. There are some farming matters to attend to and once these are over I'll come down. That Chuppu Pillai has been released from Tiruchi jail and has returned. I learnt from him that Athimber is very weak. He said he has occasional fever. One can't be sure how true it is as one can't believe Chuppu Pillai completely. I've written a letter to Athimber and also to that respected officer, Sri Duraiswami Iyer. I'll let you know as soon as I receive any reply. If possible, I'll come over myself. Don't worry.

There's nothing else by way of news. Irangal Sub Magistrate Narasimha Mudaliar died four days ago. They say he tried to molest a Muslim woman and four Muslims got hold of him, beat him to death and left his body at his own doorstep. After a postmortem, the doctor has given a report of death by unnatural causes. But nothing can be proved. Don't talk about this or spread the news. Your teacher Rajagopala Iyer has moved to a job in Madurai with a salary of seventy rupees a month. I enclose a letter from Padmi. I don't know what she's written. She didn't want me to read it and sealed it before giving it to me. No other news.

With blessings and seeking Lord Subramanya's grace,

Ayyavier

As he finished reading this out his mother said, "Appa Nanu, write to your maama at once. I'm very worried. Chuppu Pillai won't tell a lie like this, whatever the enmity. Deivamé, what more do you have in store for me? Haven't I suffered enough? Write immediately and ask Maama to make detailed enquiries. Ask him to write another letter to Tiruchirapalli."

Narayanan promised to write in time for the evening's post. Seethai Ammal forgot about Padmavati's letter and went away to attend to some work. Narayanan opened the letter which was very quaint in its spelling and punctuation. The gist was that her studies had slowed down, her parents fought often, her mother cursed her, Athai and Nanu and hit her often, and so could she run away and come to Nanu? The sentence that struck Narayanan and caused him grief was the last one – that Chuppu Pillai had told her father Athimber was dying. His instinctive reaction was to repeat this to his mother, but he thought it would upset her further and decided to keep quiet. He immediately wrote to Ayyavier, requesting him to let him know the real position. His reply to Padmi was brief – to study well, obey her mother, remain at home and not think of running away.

Though under sixteen Narayanan, unlike other youngsters of his age, was not flippant by nature. Apart from being a keen and intelligent student, the tribulations he had suffered at that young age had been a test by fire and had brought out some sterling qualities in him.

Narayanan, who followed Gopalan upstairs, came down after a while calling out to his mother anxiously.

Six brahmin boys ate in Seethai Ammal's house, each paying six rupees a month. Besides, Seethai Ammal sold homemade snacks, and was thus able to earn enough for her livelihood. She did have some reservations about this and was deeply distressed, especially when she compared this, the ignominy brought on by her husband and the tensions of making a livelihood, to the pampered childhood in her rich father's house, and the respectability she managed to maintain while living with her husband. However, she had dreams of Narayanan settling in a good job once his education was over and of a fully reformed husband returning after his release. These expectations cheered and encouraged her. She also derived considerable satisfaction at being able to show Subbammal that although her husband languished in prison, she and her son could live without any help. She, in fact, regretted not having adopted this way of life as soon as her husband was imprisoned.

It is far better to struggle for livelihood than live off someone's largesse. If one accepts charity, one becomes a slave, bound in body and soul to the donor, living according to his dictates. Of what use is one's native intelligence then? When one has to always act on another's command, one's talents and intelligence are an unnecessary burden. Food earned with the sweat of one's brow is the tastiest. A great scholar has said that an able-bodied man who does not know how to earn a livelihood does not deserve to live in his country and should be exiled. Thiruvalluvar also says that it is better for a person to die than beg for livelihood.

Not that Seethai Ammal understood all these arguments, but she derived great satisfaction from living through her own efforts, without help from anyone.

Among the young men who boarded at Seethai Ammal's house were two brothers, Gopalan and Sankaran, sons of Pannai Seshier, a rich mirasdar of Ariyur, a town some five miles from Tirunelveli. The elder of the two, Gopalan, the same age as Narayanan, was his classmate. He was married. Narayanan and he soon became very close friends. Sankaran, the younger brother, was in a lower class and was not married. He was short and stout, cunning and adept at making mischief, setting people against one another and generally promoting ill will. He had even caused a misunderstanding between Narayanan and Gopalan once and they were not on talking terms for four days. His nature had earned him the nickname "Wily Narada."

One evening, the three boys were having supper and Seethai Ammal was sitting by their side darning a sari.

She said, "Gopu, tomorrow is Saturday. Are you going home? Will the carriage come for you?"

Gopalan replied, "Yes, Amma, my birthstar falls on Sunday and I'll have to go home for my birthday. Nanu's never visited our place and would like to come along. I'm also very keen on it. Could he come, please? I'd be so happy if you agree."

"Of course," said Seethai Ammal, "This is such a small desire, so easy to agree to. You'll be back on Monday, won't you?"

"Oh yes," said Narayanan. "We have school. We'll definitely be back."

After a while, Sankaran said, "I say, Nanu, do you know? You have a new title."

"What is it?" asked Narayanan.

"I wasn't aware of it. Padmanabhan of your class told me about it. Since you're from Chirukulam, and are the son of Sitapathi Iyer, you are Chi-Chi Nanu or Dog Nanu."

Gopalan was annoyed, "Sangu, you're always carrying tales. I've pulled you up time and again but you never learn. You have the title Wily Narada and that has caused you no harm. So if some rogue calls Nanu Chi-Chi Nanu, he'll ignore it. His title at least is based on his parentage. Yours is based on your nature."

"I merely repeated what Pappu told me," said Sangu. "You must rap him on the knuckles for that. Why are you trying to pick a quarrel with me?"

"There's no need to rap anyone. And I'm not trying to quarrel. Pappu is a rascal. Why do you talk to him? Why do you repeat what he said to Nanu? Did he ask you to? Are you his hired help?"

Seethai Ammal intervened, "Let it be. He has spoken out of familiarity. Nanu hasn't taken it seriously. Drop the matter."

"No Amma, that's not the point," said Gopalan. "This chap's mischief is getting from bad to worse. And he seems to have taken to it on a full-time basis. At this rate he'll surely land in prison."

The last sentence cut Narayanan and his mother to the quick and tears welled up in their eyes. Gopalan, who knew the background, regretted his slip even before the words were fully out. He was terribly embarrassed and got up to wash his hands, head bowed in shame. Sankaran got up muttering, "You'll no doubt benefit if I land in prison."

So much avoidable and unnecessary trouble results because we don't follow the advice of the kural, Guard your tongue above all. He who does not, will suffer shame and sorrow. It has been well said that while the burn from a fire may heal, that caused by a fiery tongue never will.

Narayanan, who followed Gopalan upstairs to study, came down after a while, calling out to his mother anxiously. Seethai Ammal, sitting motionless, plunged in thought, pulled herself up with a start and cried, "What is it, child?"

Narayanan was trembling all over. "I don't know, Amma," he said, "I feel so strange. My heart is thudding and I'm so cold. How can it be cold so soon? It struck five only a minute ago! I've never felt like this before. I can't describe it. I'm scared."

Narayanan's mother was also experiencing all these strange sensations even as he had called out to her. Fearing her son would be more scared if he knew what she was going through, she controlled herself and tried to calm him, suggesting that perhaps the leftover rice he had eaten was responsible for the chill.

"No, Amma," said Narayanan. "It isn't that. Gopu is not affected. See how the hair on my arms is standing up! What shall I do Amma, what shall I do?" He sat down, and his mother, trembling from head to foot, hugged him calling out to the gods, pleading with them to save her child. Tears streaming down her cheeks, she smeared some vibhuti on his forehead and her own. Had Narayanan been his normal self he would have realized that of the two of them, his mother was the more agitated.

After a while he got up saying, "It's all right now, Amma. It all seems a dream," and went back to his studies. But the strange sensation experienced by Seethai Ammal persisted. Friends, this life is but a long dream. Let us pray that it turns out to be as pleasant as possible.

At six o'clock the next evening a carriage arrived for Gopalan and party.

At six o'clock the next evening, a carriage arrived for Gopalan and party. It was a well appointed one, comfortably upholstered and drawn by a pair of shell white bullocks of superior breed, worth at least three hundred rupees, with bells around their necks and metal clasps on the tips of their sharp horns. It was a beautiful moonlit night. Since it was getting late, apart from the cartman, two guards accompanied the carriage, running breathlessly beside it, holding on to its sides.

Narayanan, who had never before travelled in such a vehicle, was both thrilled and shy. After a while, he noticed that the guards running alongside were panting. Feeling sorry for them he said, "Gopu! The moon is bright and you say your town is only three miles away. We will be reaching it in no time. Why don't you ask one of these chaps to go to the front and let the other come along slowly?" "Adé," Gopalan said to one of the guards, "Climb into the front and let Sudalaiandi follow slowly." But the maravars were firm in their refusal, "Oh no, yejaman, we are used to this. The road is not good and the bullocks are young. They can't bear much weight. We are servile puppies, let us do our duty. Periya yejaman will slaughter us otherwise."

They reached Ariyur by eight o'clock. There were two lower caste streets in that village and a quarter of the houses there belonged to Pannai Seshier. He himself lived in the main street in two houses joined to make a large two storeyed building. A screen covered the entrance which was illuminated by a large lantern. The pannaiar, sitting on a cot outside, was engaged in a discussion with his accountants and the town guards. The three boys paid obeisance to him. He enquired after their welfare and whether they had performed the sandhyavandhanam. On being told that they had done so at a pond on the way, he asked them to go inside.

A large bronze lamp lit the main hall of the house. Beside it a young woman was lying on an old silk sari. She sat up as the three entered.

She was about eighteen, not very fair but with a rare glow in her complexion. She was taller than the average brahmin woman, her figure perfectly proportioned. Her long delicate neck added beauty to the necklace she wore. Her limbs were well rounded and her waist slender. Her hair, now slightly dishevelled, reached below her waist. She had a face, neither oval nor round, of matchless beauty with dark, arched eyebrows, below which was her most striking feature – large, dark, lovely eyes. It might have been possible to describe them in normal conditions but now, awakened from a light slumber to behold her beloved brothers, their beauty and the range of emotions they displayed defied description. The glow of the large lamp dimmed in comparison to the brightness of her eyes. Her lovely lips, naturally red, were of a colour that other women could not have managed even with the aid of a stack of betel leaves and a lump of lime paste. It could be said that her figure and features were god given, but her exquisite feminine grace? Kamban, while describing the beauty of Sita, whom he had seen only with the eyes of the mind, says, The belief that Manmatha lost his bodily form because of Siva's angry gaze is incorrect. He (Manmatha) really wore himself out infatuated as he was by Sita's beauty. Could we not describe this lady similarly, lucky as we have been to be able to see her to our heart's content? One seeing her for the first time would feel sorry that unlike Ravana, one possessed only two eyes, and not twenty.

As soon as she saw her brothers, that lady asked, "Gopu, Sangu, why so late?" Perhaps there might be something in the world that could equal her beauty, but there truly was no match for the extraordinary sweetness of her voice. Narayanan, spellbound at the sight of the young woman, nearly fainted when he heard her voice. He was transported by a sort of fervour. His feelings could be compared to the ecstasy of a simple devotee of Siva, blindfolded and taken to the sanctum of Lord Nataraja at Chidambaram on the auspicious occasion of Thiruvadharai, with his blindfold removed at the precise moment of the deeparadhanai.

Narayanan was overcome with a strange emotion, a feeling of unease he had never experienced. In later life, he often wondered why he had not fallen at her feet.

"We started late," Gopalan answered his sister. "Nanu, why are you gaping? Sit down. This is my elder sister Savithri. I've told you about her, The sly minx. Well, here she is."

Savithri smiled shyly and lowering her head said, "Oh, stop it! Who is this?"

Gopalan struck a pompous pose, "I present the honourable Sri Narayanan."

"Don't be silly," said Savithri, "I got the name all right. But who is he?"

"I've told you. He's my classmate. The son of the lady at whose house we board in Sindhupoonthurai."

Sangu said, "The name is Chi-Chi Nanu," and laughed. This caused Narayanan, already very shy, to lower his head in embarrassment.

"Sangu always talks in riddles. Now what does that mean?" asked Savithri.

Gopalan said hurriedly, "Meaning? That Nanu is from Chirukulam and that his father's name is Sitapathi Iyer. An idle rascal in school coined the title and Sangu is babbling about it."

"Is that all? What does his father do? Is he in service? Agriculture?"

Sangu started, "His father? In Tiruchirapalli ..." Gopalan cut him short.

Savithri said, "Why are you so snappy? You're hungry, perhaps? Let him finish. Is he employed in Tiruchirapalli?"

Sangu continued with relish, "No, in Tiruchirapalli jail ..." when Gopalan told him sharply to stop and signalled to his sister that he would tell her later.

All of Narayanan's euphoria evaporated and tears of humiliation filled his eyes. He would have preferred to have the whole truth come out, but Gopalan's efforts to spare him the embarrassment was even more painful. When he realized Savithri would come to know about his tainted background, he felt he would die of shame. He would not have minded if at that moment, the information had been broadcast the world over, provided it did not reach Savithri's ears. Even though the crime was his father's, the thought that Savithri might think ill of him was unbearable. Pretending to scratch his nose, he wiped his tears surreptitiously, thinking desperately that death was preferable to such a life. He was very sorry that he had come to Ariyur and found himself despising everything and everyone. He even felt a surge of anger against his father. Such is the consequence of our egoistic self-importance which places a high value on the esteem of others and suffers needlessly when that esteem is affected.

Meanwhile, Gopalan's father came in, asking, "Hasn't Mappillai Sundu returned yet?"

Savithri said, "No, Appa, and it's getting so late ..."

"He'll be coming now. I asked him to look up some lands. Go ahead and start serving dinner. There, he's come."

Savithri stood up as a short, thin, dark man of about twenty five entered the hall. He greeted his brothers-in-law and made the usual enquiries. His speech showed a rather pronounced nasal twang.

After dinner, Gopalan's father left for his bungalow where, it was rumoured, his mistress joined him. Gopalan's mother had died some ten years ago. A distant relative, an indigent widow, took care of the household chores, while Savithri kept house.

Savithri's husband helped himself to some betel leaves and nuts and disappeared. The others sat in the moonlit mittam and chatted for a while before going to bed.

There was the resounding chant of auspicious mantras specified in the holy texts for a long life.

P annai Seshier's house bustled with activity the next day. There was the resounding chant of auspicious mantras specified in the holy texts for a long life. Smoke from the homam combined with that from the kitchen to fill the house. The priestly class of brahmins displayed all their skills and made most of the occasion. Some received money twice or even three times, claiming to be new arrivals. Some demanded extra payment, pretending to recite scriptures of which they knew nothing. Yet others, though in a position to give, came dressed in rags to seek payment. An old man adopted a particularly clever ruse. In the rush of the crowd, it was impossible for him to reach the host. He slyly upset the vessel of water he was carrying and when the crowd moved aside inched his way forward muttering, Ada, ada, has it spilt? spread the dirty cloth he was carrying and squatted there comfortably. In sum, the day's proceedings cost Seshier up to a hundred rupees. Many received money and everyone enjoyed the feast. The mantras chanted were in a language few understood and could well have been curses rather than blessings. Only the Almighty would have known the mistakes in the recitation.

Smoke spread throughout the house. The ladies of the house and of some neighbouring homes were hard at work. The poor kurava gypsies, the dogs and the crows of the town fought for the food on discarded dinner leaves. To cap all this, a few jewels and silks also made their way out of the house that day.

In this melee, Narayanan shook off the despondence of the previous day. Savithri was particularly kind and considerate. He found that the strange feeling he first experienced on seeing Savithri was growing more intense. It was his furtive wish that Gopalan should not know of his feelings. Yet all he wanted was to be near her and talk with her.

This was easy because, as a dear friend of her brother, she placed him on the same footing and treated him with familiarity. He considered it a great misfortune she was not his sister. He found new beauty in each of her movements and even the most casual words she spoke seemed to him to contain some sweet secret. He could not meet her eyes when she glanced in his direction but his eyes followed her continuously. It did not occur to him to take anything she said lightly. He was astonished when her brothers contradicted her or bantered with her and felt she was above such familiarities. To him, her very presence was holy and he was convinced no harm would come to anyone close to her. He looked upon her not as an ordinary mortal but as a goddess, a combination of Saraswathi and Lakshmi. He felt that while talking to her, he would not be troubled by sensations like hunger and thirst. When they accidentally brushed past each other, her jewelled armband touched him slightly steeping him in ecstasy for full five minutes.

Narayanan was very keen to know more about Savithri, about her tastes and activities, but was afraid to ask, for fear of being misunderstood. Though to him she was an incarnation of Saraswathi, the Goddess of Learning, he did not know if she was educated. To find this out, he resorted to a strategy. He asked Sangu if the town had a girls' school. When the answer was No, he asked him where Savithri had studied. The mischievous Sangu dragged him to the kitchen. "This is Savithri's school, these pots and pans and vessels are her books, and the food she serves us is the poetry she composes," he said and laughed uproariously. Narayanan refused to believe that the person he venerated as Saraswathi was actually illiterate and had to be convinced by Savithri herself. But he had little doubt that if she put her mind to it and made the effort, there would be no branch of knowledge she could not master. His devout wish was that she should achieve this and he decided to broach the subject tactfully to her and her brothers.

That night, the four of them sat chatting in the moonlit mittam. Savithri, though tired with the day's exertion, put off going to sleep, as her brothers were to leave the next morning.

Gopalan said, "This time tomorrow night Nanu and I would be studying in his house."

"And I'd be fast asleep," said Savithri.

Considering this the opportune time, Narayanan said, "Why do our people feel that only men should study and that women should remain steeped in ignorance? Is this fair?"

Sangu had an answer. "The only object of learning is to make money. Our brahmins were learned in the vedas and sastras only because that provided them a living. It suited them to shut out even the sound of English, scorning it as neecha bhasha. But times have changed and they have realized the truth of the saying, Those lentils will not cook in this water. You find English learning most widespread in the families of these very learned brahmins who now refer to it as raja bhasha. Servants of Time, all of them!"

Gopalan laughed. "Not bad. Sangu is turning out to be quite an orator! Perhaps he attended the lecture at the Tamil Sangam the other day? But I feel there's another reason for studying. Even sons of the richest families are seeking education, only for the status government employment provides. Do you know why Sangu and I are studying? Only because some revenue inspector once insulted Appa. But for this, the two of us would have been into farming like Athimber and wouldn't have met you, Nanu."

Savithri sighed, "Money doesn't mean much these days. One needs an English education for distinction."

Narayanan then waxed eloquent on his theme. "I agree with what you say. Most people study for money and respectful employment. That is why education of women is considered unnecessary, because women cannot seek employment. A woman is benefited from her husband's job. She buys jewellery and silks and gains special status as the wife of a government servant. When the wives of the Sub Magistrate or the Tahsildar go out on festival days, deities are forgotten! All the lanterns are diverted to light their way and the gods are left in darkness until the ladies get tired and decide to go home. And from the police redheads and liveried guards surrounding them, one would begin to suspect that they were murderers or criminals under detention. This may be amusing, but sadly, while the crowd is being cleared, so many get pushed, beaten and crushed. The point is that if education is valued only for the status it brings, women's education is really unnecessary. The true purpose of learning has to be correctly understood, otherwise the importance of women's education will never be understood."

Savithri was impressed. "Why! Narayanan is quite a pandit! Even the missionaries who lecture on some Sundays aren't so fluent. But do tell us, what is that real reason?"

Her praise embarrassed Narayanan, and while he paused, Sangu cut in, "I'll tell you, it is only to enable women to write love letters. It seems an educated girl of the north corresponded with her lover and eloped to Madras."

Of the north: In the context of Tirunelveli district, the North generally indicates the Thanjavur area.

Narayanan was still a little shy and said, eyes downcast, "I'm no pandit! I merely repeated the gist of a lecture on women's education my old teacher Rajagopala Iyer once delivered. Sangu's reason is silly. To say women should not be educated because they would start writing clandestine love letters is like saying that because fires are destructive, no stove should be lit in any house. Education is as important for one's character as fire is for one's comfort. Anything on earth can be put to bad use! The main benefits of education are development of our native intelligence and faculties and understanding of basic ethical values. Money and status are secondary. Only if you accept this can you understand the importance of women's education. A woman derives benefit from her husband's earning but not from his learning. She may be able to buy jewellery with her husband's money but little else. Can a husband eat for his wife too? Similarly, one cannot study for another. Education is essential for developing one's personality and the awakening of one's intelligence, which alone differentiates us from animals. Remember the kural, The learned are the only ones truly endowed. The rest have no real possessions.

"There is also another reason. Children in our society are wholly in the care of women until their teens. Isn't it important that educated and enlightened persons guide these impressionable young minds? And then, if the wife is not educated, how will she establish true rapport with her husband who happens to be educated, learned? To quote a kural again, True conjugal happiness does not come from a physical relationship but from genuine mutual understanding. There should be a sound base for a couple's compatibility."

A MADHAVIAH

Warming to his theme, Narayanan grew more eloquent. "Disparity in education can be a great handicap. Now, if Gopu and I were enthusiastically discussing something we had read in English, and you Savithri were to ask, What's so interesting?, we'd say, You won't understand, it's in English. You'll be denied that enjoyment. A wife keen on retaining her husband's love and affection through life, even as she ages and loses her looks, should try to share his interest in learning. A husband will respect only such a wife. Otherwise he'll begin to ignore her ideas and wishes."

Sangu had gone to sleep, leaning against the wall. But Savithri and Gopalan listened with growing interest and excitement. When Narayanan finished, Gopalan patted him on the back, "Brilliant! We thank our distinguished speaker."

Savithri was thrilled. "I've made up my mind," she said a little shyly. "I won't care if anyone makes fun, I'll start studying from tomorrow. And Nanu, when you come with Gopu again, you can judge my progress."

"Brave words," said Gopalan. "If Athimber comes to know about your attempt, he'll start using a stick on you, not just his hands."

Savithri was not to be deterred, "He won't mind. In any case, he doesn't even have to know about it. I'll get Shala or some schoolboy to start me on the Tamil primer. Shala has been urging me to do this for a long time."

Her brother was still skeptical. "But of what use will that be?" he asked. "Is learning to read and write Tamil going to lead to the sort of enlightenment the honourable Narayana Iyer lectured about? If you really want to study, you'll have to acquire a BA or MA in English."

"No, Gopu, that's not right," said Narayanan. "In our society that level of education can be attained only by a few men right now.

Who knows how many aeons it will take for women to reach that stage? To say that there's no point in studying if one can't reach that level is a bit extreme. Something is always better than nothing. Don't you know the saying, A half paisa chain is better than a bare neck? Tamil may not provide guidance to all the sciences, but its literature is wonderfully rich, and can raise one to higher levels of thought. My teacher Rajagopala Iyer often used to say that no language possesses the equivalent of the *Thirukkural*, that the thrill of the Thevaram cannot be matched by any religious poetry, and that the lyrical beauty of *Kamba Ramayanam* has few equals. This is not widely known only because the English are ignorant of our literature. So much pleasure and benefit can be derived from studying such texts. Our women should learn not to waste time gossiping or singing silly songs. They could learn much even by reading the legends of heroines like Chandramati, Sita and Damayanti."

Savithri said, "Gopu is used to snapping everything I say into two and throwing it aside. But I don't care. I'm certainly making a start tomorrow. But it's very late. Sangu's been asleep for ages. Let's go to bed."

Sangu, woken up, babbled, "Was it I who said there was not enough salt in the avial?" which set everyone laughing as they went to bed.

That night Narayanan dreamt of teaching Savithri.

The famous astrologer, Anthaneri Raghava Iyengar, thought deeply and consulted many palm leaf texts.

Three months had passed since the events of the last chapter. Narayanan's father had died in Tiruchirapalli prison. What was remarkable was that the death occurred the day prior to Narayanan's departure for Ariyur, and around the time he and his mother experienced strange sensations and a feeling of doom.

During the vacation Narayanan and his mother were in Chirukulam to help arrange a marriage for Padmavati. Because of the recent death of his father it must be clear to all that it was not Narayanan whom Padmavati was to marry. But then, who else? Padmavati was now ten. Though her father Ayyavier had tried very hard, he had not been able to find a suitable match. Finally, when he was on the point of settling for Narayanan, came the news of his father's death, and that scotched the idea. Padmavati's mother was concerned about her daughter's physical development, that she would reach puberty in a year, and so a quick marriage was very necessary. At the same time, she was determined that Narayanan, with no means of his own, should not wed her daughter. With no prospect of any suitable match, she insisted that Kittu, son of her athaan Anantarama Iyer of Irangal, should be the bridegroom. No one thought of ascertaining Padmavati's opinion. But why had she to be asked? Was it not her duty to accept whatever her parents decided, marry the man of their choice and slave for him for the rest of her life? The question of mutual compatibility, if at all considered, was a concern of the parents. How could a young girl be expected to know her own mind?

Padmavati now had to accept Kittu, whom she had teased from childhood as Kari Kittu, and Thadi Kittu, as her lord and master, looking upon him as Manmatha, the acme of male beauty. If she found this difficult, she had only to take it as ordained by fate and not express any opposition. Did not adjustments always emerge over time? Were not misunderstandings and quarrels between husband and wife a daily occurrence? That was the way of the world and not worthy of consideration when a good alliance was on hand. What of marriages arranged ignoring compatibility that worked out? Take Nani, for example, whose bitter, noisy quarrels with her husband were a daily feature. Idle talk about this and her seeking solace with Subbier, her paramour, has to be ignored, since people look upon gossip as their main occupation. But then, does Nani have anything to complain about? She lives comfortably, with a house full of children. Everything is decided by fate. Is there anything we can do?

Ayyavier decided to act according to his wife's wish and tentatively fixed an auspicious date for the wedding before consulting the famous astrologer Anthaneri Raghava Iyengar with the horoscopes. That expert thought deeply, consulted many palm leaf texts and then pronounced that the groom lived near the bride's home, that he was related to her through her mother, that he was elder to her by only a year, that Padmavati could never marry anyone else as this was the match ordained by the heavens, and that even if no action was initiated, the marriage would take place with certainty within a fortnight, that is, by the eighth of Chithirai. This pronouncement dispelled most of Ayyavier's misgivings and he presented Iyengar, with appropriate ceremony, a pair of veshtis and three rupees and invited him to grace the function with his presence. On returning home, he sought to eliminate some nagging doubts by flower choice at the feet of the

---

Flower choice: Divine approval of a decision interpreted through the type or colour of a flower picked up with closed eyes in the sanctum of a temple.

local deity. When that too was favourable, preparations for the wedding of Padmavati with Chiranjeevi Krishnan, son of Irangal Anantrama Iyer, started in earnest with the setting up of the pandal, collection of necessary goods, ordering of jewellery, despatch of invitation letters and the like. Two muhurthams were selected, for the eighth and tenth of Chithirai.

Suppressing her grief, Seethai Ammal worked with dedication, as if for her own son's wedding. Narayanan's reactions were mixed, but he concluded that on the whole it was providential he was not getting married then, in the interest of his studies. As for Padmavati, her personal feelings continued to be disregarded but a great deal of fuss was made in dressing her up. Her hands and feet were decorated with henna and she was laden with jewellery of every type, design and make from head to toe. These clanged and jangled as she moved about and the sounds seemed to echo her inner turmoil. She was wrapped in a thick, heavy sari twenty cubits long, two cubits broad and two and a quarter tulams in weight, and which had never come in contact with water of any kind other than her sweat.

Her father nursed a regret that the age difference between the bride and the groom was not enough but her mother, whose joy knew no bounds, was delighted with her little son-in-law.

Ayyavier's assets totalled only about five thousand rupees. He was keen that the wedding of his firstborn should be a grand affair, and decided to spend up to two thousand rupees, proceeding to raise the money by mortgaging some of his lands. His budget was as follows:

Wedding Expenses	Rupees	Annas	Pice
Pandal	100	0	0
Food and expenses on account of priests	500	0	0
Music, dance and pipes	500	0	0

Dresses, clothing, et cetera	200	0	0
Jewellery for the groom	200	0	0
Jewellery for the bride (Apart from Rs 500 worth gifted by her in-laws)	400	0	0
Incidental expenses	100	0	0
Total	2000	0	0

And so, with due pomp and ceremony, on the evening of the seventh of Chithirai, the bridegroom, Chiranjeevi Krishna Iyer, arrived in a palanquin in procession from Irangal, to the accompaniment of pipes, drums and dances by nautch girls. The bridegroom's party of about fifty decided to walk the short distance, sending their goods by bullock carts. The preliminary vratham was performed that evening followed by thamboolam for the whole village. The muhurtham was fixed for twelve noon the next day.

The groom, a young boy after all, could not resist temptation and gorged himself on sweets and mangoes. The next morning he had indigestion and slight fever. Appropriate medicines were given and the ceremonial bath was substituted by a token sprinkling of holy water. It was decided to go ahead with the ceremony. But the fever rose rapidly and the boy became delirious. The apothecary of Irangal was sent for. Examining the patient he said he should have been called in the first place, as the barber's medication had aggravated the symptoms. He administered one dose of medicine and promised to send three more. As soon as he left, some old widows got together and declaring English Medicine was too heat generating and unsuitable for swadeshi constitutions, insisted that a Renowned Medical Pandit, a barber in Irangal, be brought. The apothecary's medicine was thrown out.

The muhurtham was postponed to the tenth.

The next morning, the famed medical pandit was brought by carriage. A doddering old man of about seventy, grey with age, his head constantly shaking under a huge turban that could easily be mistaken for a washerman's bundle, he felt the patient's pulse on both wrists for a long while and proclaimed, "This is a three day visitation of a little devil whose power will last only till tomorrow evening. It has thrived on the wretched medicines given and grown ferocious. Had you sent for me straightaway, I would have tamed it completely by now. So what? I will control the donkey and snuff it out with just two doses. Are any of these saniyans unknown to me? Is there any such donkey not tamed by me? Just wait and watch. Can they fool around with me?" Administering a pill dissolved in buttermilk, he said that the carriage be sent to fetch him again that evening, and accepting thamboolam, demanded three rupees for decocting a sanjivani oil and left.

The fever increased, the patient's condition worsened and relatives crowded around the sick bed, blocking the passage of fresh air. The noise, the weeping and wailing increased. Many new medications were tried as suggested by various people.

But all to no avail. At eight o'clock on the morning of the tenth, the date set for the wedding, Kittu departed from this world. The pandal set up for his wedding was used for his funeral. The anguish and gloom that filled the house and indeed the entire village was a tale of unrelieved sorrow.

While Gopalan and Narayanan were returning from school one evening, Savithri's name cropped up.

While Gopalan and Narayanan were returning from school one evening, Savithri's name cropped up. After some hesitation, Narayanan used this opportunity to enquire if she had actually started on her studies. Gopalan said, "Oh, I forgot to tell you. She started very recently and can now write better Tamil than me! Seems like she is always at her books. I don't think Athimber is aware of this. She has a friend called Shala, wife of the Canal Superintendent Nagamier. I think she is from the north. She, it seems, knows Tamil very well. The two study together and when doubts arise, that girl consults her husband. They're able to use Nagamier's large collection of books. Savithri has already overtaken me in Tamil. Hereafter, I'll have to ask her to clarify my doubts. Remind me when we get home. I'll show you her letter."

Narayanan was delighted. "Didn't I tell you? I knew it. If she's taught English, she'll pick it up equally fast. Don't you recall the verse, They make light of tribulations, forget sleep and hunger, brush aside impact on others, ignore cost and even insults, who have their attention focused solely on the task in hand."

Once home, putting down their books Gopalan suggested a walk to the riverbank. Narayanan said eagerly, "But you said you'd show me Savithri's letter."

Gopalan took the letter out from his trunk, saying, "A couple of personal matters are mentioned. But I don't mind your reading them. She's mentioned you too."

Narayanan turned the letter over, "Well, four pages! The handwriting is very well formed indeed." He started reading.

Ariyur, Monday.

To my dearest brother Gopu,

We are all well here. I hope you, Sangu and your friend are well. You must surely write to me every week without fail. Please note that I'm dead serious about this and act accordingly.

Gopalan and Narayanan laughed over this.

The main reason why I haven't written to you for so long is that Visalakshi and I have been reading *Purandharan Kalavu Maalai*. It has been a great pleasure but has also caused some laziness. Besides, it's hard enough to find time to read on the sly, let alone write letters! Have you read this book? If you want to, I'll ask for it to be sent to you. It's an excellent book, written by the poet Puhazhendi, the author of *Nala Venba,* while he was in prison.

Actually, I wanted to write to you about something else. There has been a lot of talk for the past ten to fifteen days of Appa's intention to remarry. But nothing has been said at home. I asked your athimber but he only snapped at me. Ayyasami vathiar has been staying in our house for the past ten days. Why, I don't know. I didn't ask Appa. How could I? When things get clearer, I'll write to you.

In any case, there's sure to be another wedding soon. Your father-in-law's brother came yesterday to give us the good news that your wife has come of age. We're all setting out now for pittu.

At this point, Gopalan inclined his head shyly and Narayanan said, "Oh, is this what you meant? Why did you try to hide it? Oh no, where are our sweets!" and proceeded to read further.

So your rutu santhi will take place soon. I think Sangu's marriage will also be settled this year. We'll know more with time. Nothing else to write about. Do reply soon.

Your loving sister

Savithri

Tuesday

We'll be leaving shortly for your in-laws' place. I've asked Shala to give this letter to her husband for posting. He corrected what I'd written earlier. He's a very nice man. He gives me books and encourages me to read. At night after dinner, once Appa leaves for the bungalow and your athimber goes out, he sends Shala to study with me. Once we had some doubts. Appa and your athimber were not at home. He came to our house, sat on the front thinnai and explained what we could not understand. But I was too shy to talk to him and hid myself. It is only because of him that I've been able to make this progress in my studies. But whenever I pick up a book, I remember what your friend Nanu said the other night about women's education. I hope he and his mother are well.

Savithri

Rutu santhi: The celebrations after the coming of age of the child bride, which marks the beginning of the couples' life together as man and wife. **Pittu**: A kind of sweet distributed to friends and relatives when a girl comes of age.

The pleasure this reference to him should have given Narayanan, was not reflected on his face. Instead, he looked slightly gloomy and was silent for a while, looking down at his big toe poking the ground. Turning to his friend he asked suddenly, "Gopu, when will you be going to your village? Only for your nuptials?" As he asked the second question, Narayanan smiled in spite of himself.

Gopalan laughed, "Don't tease! Don't you remember that we took a vow not to agree to an early nuptial after we had heard Sundaram Iyer's lecture on child marriage? At any rate, I've decided to wait until I pass my FA. But why do you ask? I'll probably go home this Sunday."

Narayanan was caught off guard, "Nothing much, really," he said. "It's some time since I visited your home and would like to go with you." His friend replied, laughingly, "Oh no, impossible! There'll be no room for you in the carriage!"

Dear reader, you may have seen many marvellous sights in foreign places or read about them in books. Astonishing new discoveries come with the passage of time. Our ancestors would not even have dreamt of steam propelled transport like trains and ships. If a great seer, gifted with the ability to foresee the future, were to tell us about the discoveries and developments to follow in the next couple of centuries, we are sure to dismiss him as a madman. Time, the architect, has immeasurable dreams and surprises in store. Even so, the most wonderful of all things, one which has persisted since the beginning of the human race, one which makes you and me and all the rest slaves of its whims, is the human mind. Do you know of anything more wonderful or surprising? Pause a while to consider the nature of the human mind, and you will readily agree there is nothing more astonishing. Thayumanavar, the eighteenth century poet, understood this very well and spoke of it with feeling in the following verse.

> One can tame a rogue elephant, A wild bear or even a tiger,
> Ride on a lion's back, Play with a serpent,
> Transmute the five metals to saleable stuff, Walk on fire, even on water,
> Get the devas to serve one, Roam around invisibly,
> Remain young forever, Enter the body of another,
> Attain unequalled siddhis, But to rein one's thoughts and still the mind,
> Is impossible, oh Pervader of my senses, My Lord.

Consider where the antics of Narayanan's mind are leading him! His Harishchandra-like mind would not let him tell a lie to save his father resulting in the latter's imprisonment. Well, may truth prevail! The law of ethics decrees that people should resort to truth without thinking of the consequences. Even if it results in an immediate wrong or discomfort to someone, it should be regarded as a blessing in disguise. People who believe in the truth must never resort to falsehood. That is only right.

But look carefully. His mind, which valued truth more than his father's welfare, took recourse to a flimsy excuse to hide from his dear friend Gopalan the rush of emotions he felt when he first saw Savithri. Now he goes further lying blatantly, trying to hide a whole pumpkin in a plate of rice, saying he would like to go to Ariyur only because he has not been there for quite some time. Was that the truth? Would that mind, suddenly, without reason, sprout such a petty wish? Let that be. Let us pose another question. Did the Gopalan mind believe what the Narayanan mind made him say? Not at all. It surmised that the reason was something else and would eventually surface. Why then did he not question his friend? Only because Gopalan was afraid that Narayanan might be offended thinking he did not want to take him along. Is this what true friendship is all about? Anyway, one should not probe too deeply in such matters. Furthermore, even if he had taken the liberty and asked for an explanation, there is no doubt that the Narayanan mind would have found some excuses and not let the truth out.

Friends, note how even the most honest of men at times deviate from the truth to satisfy the base instincts of selfishness, self-esteem and egotism, sacrificing their innate wisdom. Just as even a stone wears away with the continuous crawling of ants, good sense is replaced by evil from small beginnings. As one gets used to it, the earlier disgust for evil is subdued and the mind reconciled. A mind hesitant to steal a plantain leaf gradually dares to commit major thefts and even murders. A mind hesitant to lie to save one's own father, may, as it gets used, rely on lying as a means of livelihood. A mind hesitant even to look closely at one's own wife in the presence of others, will, as it gets steeped in evil, dare to forcefully drag another's wife by the hand in broad daylight. There is a tale of a Vishnu bhakta who once went to Tirupati. At the first sighting of the hill, he was awed by the sheer height, and for the first two days worshipped his god from the foothills. Later, overcome with desire, pausing and resting often, he managed to reach the temple with difficulty. And now, he goes up every morning, has his darshanam and returns to the town at the foothills for lunch. He is neither awed nor do his feet ache. The climb is no longer a feat for him. He is in fact surprised at his initial hesitation and awe.

Reader, your mind and mine, Narayanan's mind and Gopalan's and the mind of all others, may differ in many ways but is vulnerable to habit, good or bad. Hence let us be very careful and watchful.

But most unexpectedly, Gopalan's brother-in-law
arrived with a carriage on Friday evening.

Narayanan and Gopalan planned to leave for Ariyur on Sunday. But most unexpectedly, Gopalan's brother-in-law arrived with a carriage on Friday evening. Gopalan, who thought business had brought him to Tirunelveli said, "Welcome, Athimber! What a pleasant surprise? I was thinking of hiring a carriage but now you've arrived with one. What's the news?"

"Good news, indeed. Now, you have to start immediately. There's no time to lose. A lot of work has to be done after we reach home. Your rutu santhi muhurtham has been fixed for tomorrow. Your in-laws would all have arrived by now. I came to Tirunelveli to make some purchases. After sending the clothing and other things with the accountant, I came over to fetch you. Narayana Iyer, get ready. You have to come too. Where's Sangu?"

Gopalan said, "Why this hurry? It sounds as if you'll proceed with the function even without me!"

"It's all because of your father. He wants to go north and so the function has to be performed before that. Don't delay. Get started!"

And so they all set out as soon as Sangu returned. When they reached Pannai Seshier's house, it was bustling with the activities preparatory to a wedding. Cries of "Mappillai has arrived!" welcomed them. There was the usual exchange of greetings, formal salutations, lighthearted banter and the like. It was around midnight by the time Gopalan and Narayanan had dinner and went to bed. Nevertheless, they chatted for a long while.

Gopalan said, "You may tease me but I honestly assure you that I'm not in the least happy about this hasty arrangement."

"I don't know about all that!" said Narayanan. "This might be your personal feeling. All I say is, your resolve has vanished into thin air."

"But what can I do? Tell me, what would you have done in my place?"

"Me? I would be aware of this. Nothing is more false than knowing that a certain step is wholly wrong and harmful, resolving to desist from it but ultimately taking that very step."

"It's all very well to lecture. But if this were to happen to you, you'd understand the difficulty."

"Don't say that!" said Narayanan. "Remember, I didn't stray from the truth even when it was a question of imprisonment for my father."

(More hypocrisy here. We all know that Narayanan is not always a shining example of honesty and that Gopalan is not entirely unhappy about the early arrangement of his rutu santhi.)

Gopalan persisted, "Tell me. What would you do in this situation. Shall we run away?"

"A fine suggestion indeed! People would think that the mappillai is slightly crazy! Is this the right time and place to start considering what you should do?"

"But what could I do? Everything happened only this evening. Do I now look to my convictions or heed my father's wishes?"

Narayanan came up with a balanced evaluation. "It isn't fair to blame you. We all face this conflict. If we were like our forefathers, things would have been easier. English education has given us new ideas about the harmful aspects of old, established practices. Hence the dilemma. Do we act to please our parents who brought us up and gave us that education? Or do we follow the principles the new education has taught us? By doing so, we would not only prove ourselves selfish, but also cause mental agony to our parents in their old age and earn their curses. We're forced to make compromises, go against our conscience and lose self-respect, while the education we have received with such difficulty, becomes meaningless and hollow. On the whole, no end of botheration is caused by this English education. This dilemma is also the real reason why our nation, though under a civilized rule, is unable to make steady progress. But I do believe the situation will improve with time, and good sense will prevail. But until then tensions are unavoidable."

Gopalan said, "It's easy to say this. I too can give a good lecture on the evils of child marriage. The problem arises only when you have to translate precepts into practice."

"All right, I give up," said Narayanan laughing. "Go to sleep now. You'll have to stay awake tomorrow night also." It was nearly dawn when the friends finally slept and we cannot say with certainty that Gopalan did not have sweet dreams about his wife.

A handsome young man dressed in a vannan washed zari veshti and uppada angavastaram arrived after a while.

The next day's function was a grand success. Though it had been arranged in haste in just four or five days, priests came from afar merely on hearsay, as promptly as if summoned by reply paid post. There was no smoke in any other kitchen of the town that day, save those of one or two sworn enemies of Pannai Seshier, whose only grouse against him was his success and wealth.

After his ritual bath, Gopalan was decked in silk and zari, with sandal paste and kumkumam on his forehead and sweet scented jasmine in his hair. He wore jewellery too — a double stranded waist chain over his silk veshti, a jewelled pendant strung on his golden punul, the sacred thread, a pearl necklace intertwined with a flower garland, diamond earrings and gem studded rings. Gold bracelets accentuated his youth and natural charm. The kohl, applied by Savithri, made his eyes appear more beautiful than hers. With lips reddened by the juice of the betel chewed and a complexion aglow with shy happiness, he looked enchanting, like Manmathan with his body restored.

His wife Kalyani was a lovely twelve year old. Fair and slight of build, she looked more like a child who should have been playing with toys and games like chozhi, ammanai, marapachi or pallankuzhi than a young woman about to assume the role of wife and head of a household. She was an equal match in the matter of ornaments. It is impossible to describe the jewellery she wore. Was she not the darling daughter of Pannai Muthier, who had provided a mortgage of rupees seventy thousand on the Neelakkaattu Mitta lands? Need we say more?

Narayanan had some strong views on jewellery in general and their use by men in particular. He was firm on never wearing any jewellery. His mother Seethai Ammal wished that, though jewelless now, he should at least wear earrings at his marriage, and sought to keep the holes in his ears open by plugging them with cloves every now and then. But he stubbornly threw away the cloves and in time the pierced holes closed up. Some of his enemies said that his denunciation of jewellery was a case of sour grapes. But then who would believe enemies? Gopalan too shared his friend's views because of association. In his case at least, it was not for lack of means. He told Narayanan that though he hated jewellery, he had agreed to wear them to please his father and sister. If we secretly examine Gopalan's thoughts, another reason becomes evident, and that is to dazzle his unlettered wife, incapable of appreciating her husband's enlightened views.

With Gopalan engaged in rituals, Narayanan was free to follow some of his ideas. He tactfully talked Sangu into keeping him company and answering his questions. He particularly wanted to know the identity of some of the guests at the function. A handsome young man of about twenty five, dressed in a vannan washed zari veshti, muslin shirt and uppada angavastram arrived after a while. Such was his appearance that even the old hag in the kitchen would have concluded without hesitation that he was an English educated government official. Else, would he wear ritually unclean, washerman washed clothes, or a chandu pottu on his forehead? Without a government job, how could he have sported whiskers or acquired Tiruchirapalli footwear or a silver wristwatch? And would a liveried peon have accompanied him otherwise? He was given a special welcome and served extra thamboolam.

Narayanan craftily asked Sangu if this was the Tahsildar.

Sangu replied, "No, the Tahsildar, the Sub Magistrate and the Police Inspector are all expected in the evening. This is the Canal Superintendent, Nagamier."

Some of our friends might wonder if it was at all possible that such a minor functionary, drawing fifteen rupees as salary, should receive so much respect and attention in the home of the lakshathipathi landlord Pannai Seshier. But those even slightly familiar with village life and customs as well as the ways of the world will have no such doubts. While the existence of almighty god is acknowledged, is it not still a practice among some ignorant persons to forget His grace and offer worship and sacrifice to imaginary spirits – Sudalaimadan, Muniandi, Karuppannan, Mari and the like? Similarly, the Governor and the Collector are but remote authorities to villagers, known only by hearsay, without day to day contact and hence ignored. On the other hand, minor officials of small stature like the Revenue Inspector, the Canal Superintendent and the Police Head Constable, whose presence is palpable and who can make or mar their daily lives, receive much respectful attention and adulation.

When Nagamier left, Narayanan quietly got up and followed him to identify his house. A little later, he went and sat down on the thinnai of that house. Nagamier also came out and sat down on the opposite thinnai and a casual conversation began, with enquiries about Narayanan's name, home, et cetera.

Nagamier, given to a pompous and slightly stilted style of speech, asked, "Is it perhaps that you and the son of this Seshier are engaged in studies together?"

Narayanan said that they were both in the same school and would appear for the matriculation examination that year.

Nagamier said, "Good, and so let it be. Is there not a younger brother also studying?"

"Yes, Sangu is in a lower class."

"Is that so? And there is another brother as well? Or perhaps it is a sister?"

Narayanan smiled. "Are you teasing me? You belong to this place and ask *me* questions! Yes, there's an elder sister."

"I'm not given to easy friendships. There are ever so many idiots and worthless chaps around. I keep myself aloof. So, it's an elder sister? Would that be that tall young woman? (Nagamier's height was not less than six feet.) Ah, and there's yet another person, a short man. Could that be another son? No? Oh, son-in-law? Well, I know only Seshier, and that too casually. It is rumoured that he is getting married again next month." Nagamier stopped at that and called out, "Who is there? Shala?"

A pert young woman came out of the house, with a saucy swinging gait that even a prostitute would have envied. "You called?" she said.

"Yes, get me that book from over there."

She then brought a small book, handed it to Nagamier, threw a flirtatious glance at Narayanan and returned inside. Nagamier turned the pages of the book, pretending to read but kept up the conversation, mainly asking questions about Gopalan's family.

Narayanan finally said, "May I see that book?" It bore the title *Varunakula Adithan Madal*, not familiar to him and seemed replete with references to women and their physical attributes. Many such portions were underlined in blue. On the first page was a brief verse written by hand, which, though in the form of an address to a goddess, was actually a thinly disguised declaration of infatuation.

Below the verse, at the bottom of the page, was written in very small, almost imperceptible letters, "To the matchless Sa...ri." Narayanan was deeply shocked. It was, as the saying went, as if a demon had emerged while starting to dig a well. But he kept his feelings under check and casually turned the pages of the book, continuing the conversation. Finally he returned the book and left, saying, "I can't follow this. It is getting late. Gopu will be looking for me."

Back in Seshier's house, he told Sangu that he had roamed the town and now had nothing else to do since the others were very busy. As he had not brought any books, would Sangu kindly ask his sister for some reading material on his behalf? Sangu brought him two books which Narayanan took upstairs for careful examination. One of them was the *Tale of Purandharan's Theft*. The title page bore Nagamier's name, followed by a suggestive verse. On another page was written an even more explicit couplet about the worthlessness of a husband not after a woman's heart. The other book was Arunachala Kavi Rayar's musical compositions on the Ramayanam. A padam, similar in content, was inscribed on the last page. The doubts that had crossed Narayanan's mind when he had first read Savithri's letter were now confirmed. He was sure that Nagamier was using his wife to exploit Savithri's eagerness to study, sending her books with messages declaring his infatuation. It is human nature to judge others by one's own standards. Narayanan understood well the reaction Savithri's looks would cause in any man, himself having come under her spell at first sight. He thought all men who beheld her would fall in love with her instantaneously. But he knew that Savithri herself was totally guileless and incapable of understanding Nagamier's approach. He was also sure that if she found out the truth, she would fling the books at his face and renounce his wife's friendship, besides informing her father and ensuring appropriate punishment. A fresh doubt crossed his mind. Was it possible that Nagamier's wife did not know about his ideas? What was Shala like? Women were not to be trusted, especially northern women. Shala certainly did not look the traditional housewife from a decent family. No one in Ariyur knew anything about Nagamier and Shala, and it was possible she was not his lawfully wedded wife but his mistress. In that case, she could actually be abetting him. Several doubts crossed Narayanan's mind.

His first thought was to discuss the matter with Gopalan. But he knew that this would rouse uncontrollable anger in Gopalan, given his deep love for his sister. Savithri's secret would then be out in the open, and apart from her studies coming to a halt, it would also affect her relations with her husband, already known to harass her. He would undoubtedly hold her guilty and be more cruel towards her. Further, the matter reaching Seshier's ears would result in large scale ruckus. All this would occur even though nothing untoward had actually happened. If some development did occur, it would best be kept secret. Circumstances had created an awkward situation and unnecessary publicity would only bring shame to all concerned. Narayanan knew it was not possible to let Savithri know. He thought over the future course of events. Now that his rutu santhi was over, Gopalan would soon set up house with his wife in Sindhupoonthurai and Savithri was sure to go over to keep Kalyani company. Besides, if Seshier were to remarry, Savithri would certainly shift, either to Sindhupoonthurai or Karuvanur, her husband's village. At any rate, Savithri would leave Ariyur soon. So, concluded Narayanan, it was best to keep his doubts to himself.

Ayyavier did some shopping in Tirunelveli the next day.

Gopalan, Narayanan and Sangu returned to Sindhupoonthurai on Monday morning. Gopalan's in-laws took his wife back to their place. He could not accompany them because of his studies. Narayanan learnt from Gopalan that the rumour Nagamier had mentioned was a fact and that Pannai Seshier had indeed decided to travel north to get married. Sangu was very angry and disgusted. He was rude and snappy, looking like the proverbial monkey that had tasted ginger. Sore about being unmarried even at fourteen, he had waited patiently while his father had arranged his elder son's rutu santhi. But when his father decided on a second marriage, without any concern for his younger son's marriage, he could not bear it any more. He talked of running away to Benares and even of committing suicide.

When the three reached Sindhupoonthurai they found that Narayanan's uncle Ayyavier had arrived. He had come there to discuss Narayanan's marriage.

"Padmi is over ten," he said, "I must get her married this year. I've always wanted her to marry Nanu. It's true my wife was not willing, but she too has softened after Kittu's death, and is now reconciled to it. Once Nanu gets a job, she will be fully satisfied. Padmi, I know, wants to marry only Nanu. These days, importance is given to the wishes of the boy and the girl. After all, it's their life and they have to live happily for long. All I want is that Padmi and Nanu should not be like my wife and me!" He added, "There is also another factor. Let me be frank. My debts are rather heavy. Over five hundred rupees were wasted in that wedding fiasco last year. I can retain my self-respect only if I limit my losses. If I seek another alliance, needless show and expenses cannot be avoided, but that won't be necessary between us.

Athimber's aabdhikam will be over in Margazhi. It's sad that he's not here to witness this marriage, but such is fate! He was not destined to see it! The horoscopes match, in keeping with our wishes. But it is the union of minds that really matters. Where did the matching of horoscopes lead to last time? We must have the wedding muhurtham on the seventeenth of Thai."

Seethai Ammal expressed her wholehearted approval. "It is your wish that matters," she told her brother. "We eat the food you give and have been left in your care. Is your grief less than mine? Nanu is more of a son to you than to me. If he has come this far it's only because of you. Please go ahead."

Narayanan, inwardly delighted, said, "Why ask me? Proceed as you wish," and lowered his head slightly.

Gopalan, who was with them, said, "Amma, this fellow is pretending. He'd be very upset if you were to say that Padmavati was to marry someone else. He's even got books he intends giving her after the marriage. See, see how he smiles!"

Sangu was mortified that even the poor boy Narayanan was getting married. He went upstairs to weep in private and give way to his grief.

Ayyavier did some shopping in Tirunelveli the next day and instructed Narayanan to go to Chirukulam with his mother by the beginning of Margazhi. He invited Gopalan and other friends and left promising to write after reaching home.

His reaction was to call for a mirror, admire his new attire.

P annai Seshier, armed with enough money and escorted by Kasivasi Ayyasami vathiar, who had given him the valuable information that nubile girls were plentiful in the north and could be bought as easily as cattle in Kazhugumalai, went north to Vanjanur in Thanjavur district. Ayyasami vathiar had already negotiated for an eleven year old girl, telling her parents the groom was a handsome, issueless widower of thirty, with property worth four lakhs which the girl would inherit after his lifetime. The deal comprised five hundred rupees for immediate wedding expenses, a thousand rupees towards jewellery for the bride and another thousand for her parents. A date was also set for the wedding and the bridegroom, Seshier, and the broker, vathiar reached the bride's village two days earlier.

Seshier was running fifty and had greyed completely. The looks of his children, Savithri and Gopalan, could lead to the surmise that he too had been handsome in his youth. But no one who saw him now, pot bellied, cheeks bloated like appams, a few stray silver strands atop his head like a coconut kernel's tuft, a neck conspicuous by its absence, could ever imagine him as a bridegroom. The vathiar, well aware of this, had had him shaved, dressed him in a new twelve by six white veshti and adorned him with jewels like rings, earrings and waistband. Also, on their way, at Tiruchirappalli, he got a shirt of red flannel made for him. In his youth, Seshier had wriggled out of an appointment as district court usher by obtaining a false medical certificate at a cost of thirty rupees, only because of his disinclination to wear a shirt, turban, et cetera. And now he didn't raise any objection to the vathiar's suggestions. Instead, his reaction to the vathiar's exclamation, "Bhesh! You now look every inch a bridegroom!"

was to call for a mirror, admire his new attire and feel delighted with his appearance before proceeding to Vanjanur. Such are the antics of lust!

Vanjanur was only a hamlet. Like the abodes of the navagrahas, it had a scattering of just nine brahmin houses. The smallest of these belonged to the family of Seshier's bride. It was a mere hovel with a thatched roof, more like the chicken coop of a large Marava household. A small pandal had been put up at its entrance. When they arrived, only the women of the family were at home. Seshier all smiles, the full set of thirty two teeth visible, could hardly contain his joy at the sight of the bride, a very pretty girl, as strapping as a Pegu pony. The girl's mother, Vanja, welcoming the vathiar asked if the bridegroom was following them. Pointing to Seshier, the vathiar said, "Here's the bridegroom." These words brought all the womenfolk out and they promptly burst out laughing. We need not describe the shame and discomfiture experienced by Seshier.

Vanja said after a while, "Please don't joke. Look, my daughter has started weeping. Perhaps Mappillai will follow? And this surely is his father. You didn't tell us the truth when you said the groom had no father." The vathiar repeated that Seshier was indeed the bridegroom.

At this point, Vanja's husband, a good ten years younger than Seshier and a notorious troublemaker of the village, returned home. When it was clear that the vathiar was not joking everyone started abusing him, passing sharp comments and witticisms like, "Does this old corpse need a marriage? Does appam cheeks need an ambadaial, a wife? Pot bellied wants a belle! Look at Mappillai's shirt, Ali Bhootham will look good in it! Mappillai's silver hair can be used to make toe-rings for his bride," and the like. The bride, huddled in a corner, was sobbing bitterly. Seshier, deeply humiliated and angry, sat head bowed, like a beggar who had lost his performing monkey, tears of shame stinging his eyes. After a while, Ayyasami vathiar and the girl's father moved to the back of the house and held a long and secret discussion, while Seshier sat outside sighing deeply. Finally the vathiar came out and asked him to come in. Seshier was angry and bitter. "There's no question of going in or coming out. This will do," he said. "Let's go home, never mind the advance."

The vathiar persisted, calmed him down and took him in again. "Can you blame me?" he asked in a soft voice. "You saw all that happened. I somehow expected this. But never mind, nothing has been lost, things are under control and I've made a satisfactory settlement. All they want is another thousand. You've seen the girl, haven't you? Did I lie about her looks? Lovelier than Rambha or Tilottama! She is worth her weight in gold, if you ask me." The vathiar was indeed a very clever manipulator and understood Seshier's mind. His description of the girl made Seshier forget everything else. The extent of his infatuation could be described with an example from *Kamba Ramayanam* where the poet describes Ravana's state of mind when he heard of Sita's beauty, He forgot Karan, he forgot his sister's disfiguration, he forgot the humiliation suffered, the valour of Dasaratha's sons, he forgot his curse. Because of Kaman's arrow, he could think only of the beauteous Sita.

Seshier, bitten as he was by the love bug, lost his senses and readily agreed, saying eagerly, "One thousand? I'm even prepared for an extra hundred if necessary, but do settle the matter. I'll send a telegram for the extra money right away."

And so it was settled. They went to a telegraph office ten miles away and sent an express telegram to Seshier's manager at

Tirunelveli. The necessary amount was on hand the next day. Thus, on the date originally fixed, an old groom and a child bride were joined in holy wedlock.

They stayed there for a week, at the end of which Seshier said that his new wife should accompany him. Her people said a long journey was inadvisable as she was nearing puberty, that they would send a telegram as soon as she came of age and fix a date for the rutu santhi after which she could go to her new home. Seshier agreed and left with the vathiar, who incidentally had already despatched by money order the five per cent commission he had got from the bride's father. He travelled at Seshier's expense and received a gift from him as well.

When his father intending to remarry went to Thanjavur, Sangu's frustration and jealousy far outweighed distress.

W hen his father, intending to remarry, went to Thanjavur, Sangu's frustration and jealousy far outweighed the distress Savithri and Gopalan felt at the decision. People's comments, "Look at this old man seeking a bride when he has a grown up unmarried son," hurt like molten lead poured down his ears and made him burn with humiliation. He considered suicide by some means or the other but lacked the courage to act. Running away from home was not possible without money, and the sale of his personal jewellery like earrings, waistband, et cetera, posed risk from cheats, and suspicion of theft and could land him in jail. Finally, a wild idea occurred to him. He had often heard about missionary activities, that in Palayamkottai there were lovely, educated Christian girls, and that if he converted to Christianity, he could not only get a bride of his choice, but also well-paid employment, with the benefit of social contacts with Europeans and luxuries such as a horse carriage. He was emboldened to consider conversion. What he knew of the Christian religion or Hinduism or any other religion for that matter was not more than the musical knowledge of a stone pillar. What else could be expected of a flippant young schoolboy?

Once this idea occurred, he began to act on it by befriending a Christian boy in his class. After a few days, he began to visit the boy's home in Palayamkottai and met his sisters who, dressed in the daring new style of pavadai, blouse and dhavani, strolled about book in hand. Unlike brahmin girls they did not run away at the sight of men but were perfectly poised and conversed with charming familiarity. He was thoroughly enchanted by this new, heavenly experience and while their manners and lifestyle were completely strange to him, they caused him nothing but delight. By and by, he spoke to his friend about his idea. The boy's father, Gurupadam, a native padre, was delighted and flattered Sangu with special attention, praising him to the skies for his youthful vision and spiritual strength, all of which went straight to his head. Finally, Gurupadam escorted him to his senior, an English priest.

The Englishman patted Sangu on his back, made him sit by his side and said, "Little brother, you are very young. Even so, the grace of our Lord has descended on you. You can measure the waters of the ocean, you can count the stars in the sky, but the grace of our Lord is immeasurable. Do you realize it's a sin to worship man-made idols of stone and metal?"

"Yes, I do," replied Sangu.

"Do you believe that in order to save us sinners, our Lord was born a man and died on the Cross?"

Sangu did not know what Cross meant, but was afraid to ask lest he be considered a fool and deciding it was the name of the town where Jesus Christ died said, "Yes, I do believe."

Later, when the Dorai and the native padre questioned him about his family background, all he revealed was that he was not married, but did not mention that this was the reason that prompted him to embrace Christianity. He thought that once converted, all advantages and pleasures would accrue automatically.

After prayers at the padre Gurupadamier's house (he was actually a saanar by caste), he was served bread, butter, sugar, milk, et cetera by the padre's daughters. He lacked the courage to eat cooked food in their house. They did not press him either.

That night, Sangu slept on an upholstered sofa in the Dorai's bungalow. It was late when he went to bed and he was also mentally exhausted. He slept very soundly until woken up by the Dorai at seven the next morning. He had dreamt that his wedding had been fixed with a lovely girl of Thanjavur, that he had been asked by his father to go over immediately, and that he was looking for Gopalan to make the necessary arrangements. At this point, the Dorai shook him awake hastily saying, "Wake up, brother, and go to that room!" Woken up suddenly and still bemused by the dream, he overheard Gopalan who was speaking outside and shouted out, "Where are you, Gopu?" It was only then that he recalled the events of the previous day and, in confusion, followed the Dorai's order and went into another room.

Meanwhile Gopalan who was outside cried, "There, I can hear him! He's here, in this bungalow. Inspectorvaal, please get your men posted on all four sides. Sangu! I'm here! Where are you? Take care, saar. They may whisk him away."

Narayanan, on his own, took position at the rear entrance. At this point, the Dorai came out and an argument followed between him and those outside. Finally, he admitted that Sangu was in the bungalow but added that he had come of his own accord seeking conversion. He then brought Sangu out. Sangu couldn't restrain his tears on seeing Gopalan and Narayanan. In a flash, before any one could realize what was happening, Gopalan and Narayanan seized Sangu and bundled him into a waiting carriage with themselves in the position of guards in the front and the rear. In a matter of fifteen minutes they reached Sindhupoonthurai.

But Seshier's grief was intense. Not even for his first wife had he mourned as much as for that chit of a girl he married at the age of fifty.

Pannai Seshier heard about Sangu's escapade when he returned home after his wedding. He immediately left for Sindhupoonthurai and brought Sangu back, putting an end to his studies leaving only Gopalan at school. He then sought to arrange a quick wedding for Sangu. At first, no one was prepared to offer a girl in marriage, for fear of Sangu's conversion to Christianity. Finally, a distant relative, a poor man tempted by Seshier's wealth, agreed to give his daughter in marriage to Sangu. Even he stipulated that the wedding should take place only after two months, as his wife's delivery was due. He said he wanted to observe Sangu's behaviour in the meanwhile. It was decided to accept his proposal.

Seshier was constantly thinking of his wife. Often he considered making a trip to fetch her. Finally, he decided to do so just before Sangu's wedding and to perform the grahapravesham alongside. Sangu's wedding muhurtham was set for the seventeenth of Thai. Seshier wrote to his father-in-law that he would come there on the fourth of Thai.

On the morning of the first of Thai, Seshier received a telegram saying his wife was critically ill with dysentery, and that he should start immediately if he wished to see her alive. Seshier was shocked and distracted, to the extent of being unable even to eat. He wanted to leave immediately, but some friends prevailed upon him to wait until the next day and take Ayyasami vathiar with him. The vathiar had gone to a village some ten miles away and so Seshier sent his carriage for him, with a fresh pair of bullocks for the return trip. Worried, he was unable to sleep a wink that night. At eleven o'clock, there was a knock on the door. Seshier concluded it was the vathiar, and promptly decided to leave by the morning train instead of the one in the afternoon. He rushed to the door, stubbing his toe against the step. Unmindful of the blood flowing from the injury, he opened the door and asked, "Who is there?"

"Telegram, yejaman " said a voice.

Seshier, thoroughly shaken, slumped on the thinnai, incapable of action. After a while, he got up and lit a lamp but could not decipher the telegram, which was in English. He thought of waking up Sangu to read it but abandoned the idea, either out of embarrassment or lack of faith in Sangu's knowledge of English. He ran to Nagamier's house, woke him up and brought him home to read the telegram. It said that his wife was dead.

Even before dawn, the news spread all over town. There were sarcastic comments about how Seshier, flush with funds, had gone all the way north and bought himself a shrardha duty for five thousand rupees. Even in his own household, no one was unduly affected. Only Savithri felt sorry for him. But Seshier's grief was intense. He covered his head with a towel and lay down in a corner the whole day, not responding even to those who came to offer condolence. Not even for his first wife, who had borne him three children and shared his life and its joys and sorrows for twenty years had he mourned as much as for that chit of a girl he married at the age of fifty and a cost of five thousand, whom he had merely glimpsed for a week. The only other person genuinely affected was the telegraph peon. He had believed the telegram addressed to a man of importance would be one bearing happy tidings and, expecting a tip, had rushed from Tirunelveli at the dead of night, to no avail. Ayyasami vathiar was also a little upset, but not too much. As the saying goes, For the mahout, an elephant is worth a thousand gold coins, dead or alive. This death might have deprived him of income from auspicious events, such as Seshier's rutu santhi, seemantham, et cetera, but there was the compensation of the ceremonies following a death. Besides, he thought of the additional income that could come from arranging yet another wedding.

The vathiar was sure Seshier was obsessed with the idea of marriage, and so began making plans. If taken north once again and shown a suitable girl, Seshier was certain to lose his senses and venture into matrimony. He therefore planted in Seshier's mind the idea of visiting his wife's village to try to cut his losses, by at least recovering the jewels, and if that was not possible, to ask for the dead girl's sister in marriage instead. He worked hard to get his idea accepted. After his initial shock wore off, Seshier agreed. On the vathiar's advice, because of this death, Sangu's wedding was postponed to next Chithirai. The vathiar escorted Seshier north once again, a week after the receipt of the telegram.

Since Narayanan's wedding was set for the same date as
Sangu's, Gopalan would not be able to attend it.

Narayanan left for Chirukulam for his father's aabdhikam and his own wedding. Examinations over, Gopalan too left for Ariyur. Both friends were disappointed that since Narayanan's wedding was set for the same date as Sangu's, Gopalan would not be able to attend it, but because of their close friendship they did not make much of this.

Narayanan was very happy at Chirukulam. His only regret was the memory of his father's prison term. Padmavati was now eleven. She did not hold the promise of a beauty such as Savithri's but had a fair complexion and lovely rounded limbs. Sweet, childlike innocence and joy seemed to spill from every pore of her skin, giving her a charming, unique glow. She was a little shy with Narayanan, her husband-to-be, but because of their childhood association, Narayanan's wish and her parent's approval, she continued to spend time with Narayanan as before. In her position, other girls would have run away to hide themselves, as if from a tiger or a bear, but she was with Narayanan for at least two hours every day, learning Tamil and Arithmetic. Though she, a child, had not cultivated a taste for learning, she took to it eagerly, because she understood the great pleasure and satisfaction her education gave Narayanan. Apart from tutoring her in the Tamil moral texts, he followed the example of his old teacher Rajagopala Iyer, and read out to her selections from the great classics like *Kamba Ramayanam* and *Thirukkural*. He made her memorize selected pieces every day and believed this would help her cultivate good taste in literature. While they were thus engaged, the conversation would sometimes turn to past events and Narayanan would tease her about something she had said or done. This would cause her much embarrassment, but it was something they both enjoyed thoroughly. In private they still called each other Nanu and Padmi, but were extremely careful not to allow this intimacy to show in company.

A week before the wedding Narayanan received a letter from Gopalan, written in a mixture of English and Tamil.

Ariyur, Thai 8th

My dearest friend Nanu,

We are all well here. I trust you, your mother, your uncle and the other person are well. Do take good care of the last mentioned. So far, my time has been happily spent teaching Savithri and playing chozhi with her. But during the past week there has been a lot of bad news that has destroyed our happiness and caused us endless worry. The proverb that misfortunes never come singly has proved true in our case. In the first place, my wife has not joined me here, as you had surmised. Neither did I go to my in-laws. It had been decided that I should go to her place on the first of Thai and bring her over in time for Sangu's wedding. Meanwhile, there was a letter saying she had been diagnosed as under the spell of spirits and was being treated by some sorcerers. So I didn't go and she did not come. It is nothing much and to be frank, I'm in a way happy about it. A few days ago, we had a telegram giving the news of the death of the girl my father had married and he has gone north again. He made a laughing stock of himself with his display of grief. A respected elder of this area, he has now become a target of fun even for the scum of society. That too is perhaps not so bad. But now he has gone off accompanied by that bane of an Ayyasami vathiar, mainly responsible for getting him into the present state. Savithri and I are afraid that he'll get married yet again. What can we do? We'll have to accept our fate. Another development has capped all this, like oil poured on a burning wound. When my father left, he said that Sangu's wedding could take place only in Chithirai. Sangu, upset with this, ran away night before last taking a golusu worth three hundred rupees and forty rupees cash from Savithri's jewel box. We've learnt he was talking about going north to Kumbakonam and joining a drama troupe. Athimber has gone in search of him. Telegrams have been sent to some railway stations as well as to my father. If we get some good news before your wedding and Athimber returns, I'm planning to attend it. Savithri wants me to go even otherwise. But I don't want to leave her alone. I'll definitely come if Athimber returns. Savithri wants me to tell you that she makes kind enquires of Padmavatiammal, even though she's not acquainted with her. I add my own enquires. Please give my namaskarams to your mother and uncle. If I'm lucky, I shall meet you next week. Do reply soon.

Your dear friend,

S Gopu

PS. No news of the exams yet. I'll write to you as soon as I get to know something. Do you know how to play pallankuzhi? I am just learning. Savithri beats me in a trice.

Gopu

The two then started walking towards Chitoor, a village three miles away. All the way Seshier was deep in mournful reflection of the beautiful wife he had lost.

S eshier and the Vathiar reached Vanjanur on the morning of the third day after their departure. They entered the village with mournful faces and covered heads. Avoiding the main road they took the narrow path along the canal, the village's source of water supply. There, as they were washing their muddied feet, they saw a brahmin girl lift a pot of water on to her hip. The sight startled them, for it was clear she was the girl Seshier had married – or else another born to the same mother at the same time. On seeing them, the girl stood still for a moment, then turned and hurried away, strengthening their suspicion. Ayyasami vathiar called after her but she quickened her pace to a run, without once turning around.

After some deliberation, the vathiar asked Seshier to keep out of sight in the coconut grove adjoining the canal while he himself went to the village to make enquiries. He knew that all but one of the nine brahmin households there belonged to relatives of Seshier's father-in-law. The odd one belonged to an Iyengar, and it was this the vathiar sought, to learn through crafty enquires, the facts of the matter. About two weeks after Seshier had married his daughter, the rogue Chuppier left for Cuddalore taking along just his wife and daughter. Once there, he removed the taali Seshier had tied from the girl's neck, declared her unmarried and married her off to Vakil Annasami Iyer in exchange for five hundred rupees on hand. The girl had come of age a week later and the rutu santhi was duly celebrated. She was now pregnant and at her father's house for the pre-childbirth ceremony of valaikappu.

So the letter and telegram were deliberate fabrications of the rogue Chuppier. At first the vathiar was really upset with these revelations, but after deliberation, decided happily it mattered little whether Raman ruled or Ravanan, that any circumstance could be turned to his advantage and that he could make not less than a hundred out of the situation. He approached Chuppier's house boldly. A long argument followed, at the end of which Chuppier offered to pay him hundred rupees if he could take Seshier away without further ado. The vathiar agreed and got thirty rupees as surety, which he hid carefully in his person.

Then, pretending deep humiliation, he walked slowly and hesitantly into the grove, his face a picture of sorrow, and sat down beside Seshier. Though Seshier pestered him with questions, he maintained an aggrieved silence and kept sighing. Finally, with a deep sigh, he said, "What can be said or done now? What's left to say? All is lost. We've been duped. As the saying goes, yesterday's newcomer has carried away the wife of the long-awaiting husband." He came out with the story bit by bit.

Seshier was stunned to silence. Tears of shame and rage filled his eyes. After a while, the vathiar sighed again and continued, "I had told you then to take the girl home, but you agreed to their arrangement. Had we taken her along, this wouldn't have happened. But then how could we have known their evil intentions? That brahmins should stoop so low! Is this the culture of Chola land? I have travelled far – to Kasi and Nepal – nowhere have I seen such depravity! How easily he fooled us, how smoothly he talked, what courtesies and honours were extended! I had of course heard that the man was a rascal, but I thought it was said out of jealousy. How sweetly he spoke! And what hospitality and courtesy! He was all sweet reasonableness! What a cheat! But I had thought it was immaterial what sort of a man he was. It was the girl that mattered. And what a girl! You can't find the likes of her in our parts, I thought. But the atrocity! Could this sort of thing have taken place in the olden days? Any one even attempting such a thing would have been tortured to death. Now Kali is taking hold and governance is deteriorating, where can we seek justice?"

Seshier, hitherto silent, sitting with head bowed, looked up at the last sentence. "Why not? We have to get justice. Even if the girl is lost, what of the money? Did you ask him for it? What did he say?"

"Who? Chuppier?" asked the vathiar, "I went to him right away, determined to get back all our expenses, plus at least a thousand as damages, and also put him in jail if possible. But that consummate rascal had the temerity to challenge me. Do you know what he said? Oi vathiare, let the gentleman come and declare publicly in court that his wife is living with another man. Even if you shamelessly abandon all sense of propriety and make such a statement, I would swear a hundred times over that the girl married to him had indeed died and this was her sister. This entire village will stand by me. A court case is nothing for me, my son-in-law is himself a vakil and he has many High Court barrister friends. I can get not one but two to appear for me. The expense is no consideration. I have more than two thousand left from the money given by your Seshier. Can you file a case? Can you find witnesses? Let's see, let's see if you can get a single witness from this village. Can you pose a threat to me, coming to Vanjanur crossing three districts? I'll surely win the case and then file a suit for defamation that will cost your pannaiar another two thousand, and a jail sentence for preparing a false case. I swear I'll get that done, as sure as I am a man and not a widow! Don't you know you are dealing with Vanjanur Chuppier, a name feared throughout the Presidency? He set up such a scene shouting at the top of his voice, that I feared violence. I was able to pacify him only with the help of a few people, and with their support I asked him to return the jewels at least. I hesitate to repeat what he said."

Seshier, though a tiger in his own home was a cowardly cat at heart, and the narrative scared him completely, as if imprisonment was imminent. He asked tremulously, "What? What did he say?"

"Nothing much. When I asked for the jewels, he said, Jewels? Why, for allowing an old man to hold her hand, my daughter ought to receive jewellery for another thousand rupees. Forget it. If the old man is so lovelorn, I can give you something by way of consolation. The sari you gave my daughter for the wedding is already old and threadbare. My daughter has been saying it would come in handy as a spread for her baby, to be born in a few months, the dear son of Cuddalore Vakil Annasami Iyer and my beloved grandson. You may keep that if you like. It would come in handy to wipe his tears. That fellow will stop at nothing. The way he talks, jumps and shouts, the language he uses! There's really no limit to his villainy. Had you gone there, a terrible fight would have resulted."

Seshier was shamed and hurt beyond words. "Let's leave it at that," he said. "Forget the loss, take it as a debt owed in a previous birth. At least I've been spared the expenses of a shrardham. Come, get up. What can you or I do? Leave it all to destiny. He'll be punished by God. Let's just go away and not breathe a word to any one. As they say, bad dreams are not to be mentioned. What would we have done if the girl had really died? Let's believe that's really the case. Let's return home as quickly as possible. I'm very hungry and thirsty. We have sent away the carriage. We can't possibly enter this village hereafter. Let's go somewhere else and find some food."

The two then started walking towards Chitoor, a village three miles away. All the way, Seshier was deep in mournful reflection of the beautiful wife he had lost and the mortifications he had suffered.

On the seventeenth of Thai, Sowbagyavathi Kamalambal was married to Pannai Seshier.

It was three when they reached Chitoor. There was no likelihood of a meal in any home in the village. Finally, a widow offered to serve them leftover rice soaked in water for three annas each. The famished travellers readily agreed. Even bitter neem would have tasted sweet. After a quick bath and the daily ritualistic obeisance, they sat down to eat. A young girl about twelve years of age, quite pretty and with a saucy air, served them food. From the way she wore the sari it was clear she was not yet married. The vathiar noticed Seshier turning around frequently to look at her. After the meal Seshier, who was tired, drifted off to sleep on the thinnai.

Ayyasami vathiar's automatic reaction to nubile maidens supported the truth in the proverb about the instinctive ability of vultures to scent carrion. And matters were so much easier with the subject under the same roof! It was not a difficult matter to fix up yet another alliance for Seshier. After all, among us, matrimonial alliances between boys and girls who have never seen each other are settled like business transactions, even in train compartments and the market place, without the slightest consideration to the opinions of those actually concerned. In this instance, where the bridegroom and the head of the family were the same person, finding a suitable bride in the Chola country with its plenitude of maidens was no feat. Besides, the widow had little by way of assets apart from her children and her cheeky self-assurance.

The vathiar reclined in the passage and started a probing conversation with the lady who belonged to the tribe of *English* widows. She sat on a chair and talked with easy familiarity. She was only around thirty with four children other than Kamalambal, the girl who had served the meal, and was eking out a difficult living after the death of her husband, Swaminatha Iyer. She could expect a decent livelihood only by selling the girl, and offers upto eight hundred rupees were coming her way.

What followed is best reported in brief. Before the sun had set that evening, Seshier went to a telegraph office seven miles away and sent a telegram to his hundi shop in Tirunelveli to send him two thousand rupees. Unknown to him, the vathiar despatched home by money order the thirty rupees he had received from Chuppier. He wrote a letter to Chuppier, telling him to send the balance seventy directly to his home, and wrote another to his home asking them to inform him about the receipt of the amount.

On the seventeenth of Thai, on the same muhurtha lagnam originally chosen for Sangu's wedding, Sowbagyavathi Kamalambal, daughter of the Chitoor widow Kamakshi Ammal, was married to Pannai Seshier. All that Ayyasami vathiar got was his fee as officiating priest. Despite his skills, he was not clever enough to get anything from Kamakshi Ammal and had to be thankful that she spared him her own extractive tactics.

On an auspicious day at the end of Thai, Seshier and the vathiar left for Ariyur, along with Kamakshi Ammal's entire brood. Gopalan's telegram had not reached Seshier as it was addressed to Vanjanur. Hence he did not know of this and other developments. On his part, Seshier had not informed any one about his Vanjanur wife or his Chitoor marriage.

Your innocent daughter, seemingly engrossed in needlework, may actually be dreaming of that horse rider.

From all that has been implied as well as stated openly so far, it must be evident that Savithri and her husband were ill-matched. Various factors contributed to this. Firstly, Savithri's husband was quite hideous in appearance. Dark, thin, short, pigeon-chested, and as hirsute as a porcupine. Furthermore, he was not perceptive enough to appreciate his wife's virtues, her patience, kindness, generosity, innocence and compassion. He thought that all men who saw his wife would be enamoured of her beauty and fall in love with her, and because he was so ugly, she would be attracted to handsome men. This judgment followed from his own inclinations and low mentality. His appearance notwithstanding, he lusted after virtually every woman he saw, and assumed that all men were like him. Since Nagamier was aware of all this, he did not dare achieve his desire through closer association with Seshier's household. Because of such suspicions, Shorty Sundaram Iyer sought to keep his wife in check, guarding her virtue by being invariably harsh, and beating her on one pretext or the other at least twice or thrice a week. It never occurred to him that if, as he assumed, Savithri really had no love for him, such an action would only make her despise him even more. He also nursed another grievance against her. Even after living with him for five years, she had not borne him a child. It is common in the world for a beneficiary of generosity not to show gratitude or appreciation. Instead, he tends to blame the benefactor for his misfortunes. Just as the sweet rose is surrounded by thorns, Savithri, with all her beauty and goodness, had a horoscope with several adverse features which made it difficult to find a match. A number of good proposals had to be rejected on this ground and finally only Sundaram Iyer's horoscope was found suitable. Following the marriage, his fortune changed completely. His poverty, want and worries vanished. But while he enjoyed every luxury, he could not bring himself to acknowledge that all this was due to his wife. He was aware that people knew him for his true worth and sought to counteract their scorn by holding Savithri responsible for all his shortcomings, even for his lowly status before the wedding.

Apart from this, despite the beauty and sweet nature of his wife, he had a mistress, a Marava woman called Sudali – dark, much taller than him, with heavy hips, pendulous breasts and protruding teeth – quite hideous in appearance. Perpetually chewing betel, she liberally sprayed all around whenever she opened her mouth to speak, or rather bark. She was over forty and old enough to be his mother. Thus, spurning the Sridevi who was his wife, he embraced this Moodevi. He also had other ladyloves from time to time. Savithri was quite aware of all this. Indeed, there was no one in town who did not know about Sundaram Iyer's affairs.

In such a situation, it is really not necessary to seek reasons for Savithri's lack of love towards her husband. Yet she never denied him his bodily needs. She was overjoyed on the days he was kind to her. But when she approached him with love, he would spurn her with harsh words and she would turn away quietly, deeply hurt, tearful and choking with emotion. Her love for him should have vanished once he showed his true temperament. However, Savithri had one ideal firmly fixed – regardless of all the cruelty, betrayal and scorn, she would never compromise on her chastity. No, this statement is incorrect. For it was not a conscious decision on Savithri's part. Even while suffering her husband's intolerable

---

Moodevi: The elder sister of Sridevi or Lakshmi, she epitomizes misfortune and ill luck.

behaviour, the thought that she could find solace elsewhere never crossed her mind. She accepted what she considered her fate without any thought of ways to change it. Reading tales of legendary heroines like Damayanti, Sita and Chandramati only increased her devotion to her husband and strengthened her resolve. She actually derived some happiness by comparing her lot with those of such heroines. Gossip about some women of the town who had compromised their virtue only caused deep disgust and anger and it never occurred to her that she too could go astray. Her mind was so pure and innocent that she never even thought that other men might be attracted to her. In fact, she was totally unaware of her extraordinary beauty and charm. She was heartbroken with her husband's behaviour and wept in private, but never spoke about it to others. To whom could she turn when her own husband spurned her? She occasionally confided in Shala, whom she considered her bosom friend. That woman repeated these confidences to her husband, which roused in Nagamier the hope of achieving his desire one day.

The affection and love inherent in Savithri's nature, finding no outlet in her husband, expressed itself in sisterly attentions. She lavished love on her brothers and father. And now, the actions of one of her brothers and her father brought her intolerable pain and anguish. She grew thin and pale. But for the presence of Gopalan, she might have lost sanity and contemplated suicide. Just as floodwaters have to be released to prevent a tank bursting its banks, pent-up affection has to find an outlet if heartbreak is to be avoided.

Friends, let us pause and consider this. Had Savithri been blessed with a loving husband and children, she would definitely not have showered so much love, attention and care on her father and brothers. For Gopalan, his sister was indeed dear but greater now was his concern for his beloved wife and her health. And Seshier, on whom Gopalan and Savithri lavished so much affection, and who, in turn, considered them closest to his heart, now cared only for his new wife. Marriage monopolized Sangu's thoughts and Ayyasami vathiar's concentration was riveted on moneymaking, whether in weddings or funerals. Regardless of everything else, Sundaram Iyer was besotted with the Marava woman Sudali, who loved Veerabhadran. Despite deep mutual love and affection, each one has his personal desire and this dominates over all his actions and thoughts. Let us go a little deeper. We note the wondrous fact that in this wide world peopled by millions, each one of us is actually alone and self-centered. Your wife may have shared your life for forty years, but if you think you are truly united, you are wrong. Does she feel the pain in your leg or do you share her toothache? Your innocent daughter who seemingly is engrossed in domestic duties or needlework may actually be dreaming of that horse rider she saw the other day. When you kiss your little son, he could actually be thinking of the money you promised him and what he still owes the sweetmeat stall. Why, even your grandmother lying helpless in a corner has her personal thoughts. Though old and approaching her end, she is probably thinking of her beauteous youth and the jewellery she wore and how even the Tahsildar had once turned around to stare at her. Take yourself. Do you tell your wife about everything you do or think? There are different worlds swirling in your mind and mine. And our tastes differ vastly. The girl you find lovely may not appeal to me, and I may detest a dish you think is delicious. In this vast ocean that is life, each of us is a separate island, and the best we can do is to endeavour to have good relationships with the other islands around us.

Life is extremely precarious and can fill even the strongest and bravest of us with fear and trepidation. May the kindly hand of a fellow traveller support you when you stumble and you in your turn go to the aid of all those near you. In this journey of life, let truth lead the way and love be your constant companion. In the end, may you be forgiven by the merciful! In this dark universe, traversing life's journey ridden with anxieties and worries, we would be like blind men without the light of love.

Sundaram Iyer, who had gone in search of Sangu, returned on the night of the fifteenth of Thai saying he could not trace him anywhere. Gopalan left for Chirukulam the same night to attend Narayanan's wedding, promising Savithri to return immediately after the fifth day celebrations.

At around six, plant a pumpkin flower on the wall of your backyard.

Though Narayanan's wedding was celebrated without much pomp and expense, it was a pleasant and joyous function. Gopalan did not, as originally planned, leave immediately after the fifth day celebrations. As the examination results were due, Gopalan and Narayanan decided to go to Ariyur first and then let Seethai Ammal know when to join them at Sindhupoonthurai. The two left on the twenty fifth of Thai and reached Ariyur on the twenty seventh, stopping en route at Sindhupoonthurai, where they learnt of their success in the examination. Narayanan immediately wrote to his father-in-law to send his mother to Sindhupoonthurai as soon as possible with some money.

As they alighted from the carriage in front of Gopalan's house, they saw a girl sitting on the thinnai combing her hair. Gopalan was startled. She too seemed taken aback for a moment but made no move. As they entered the house, they heard an unfamiliar voice in the kitchen saying, "Chellam, there is some milk, go and drink it!" Savithri, who had heard the sound of the carriage, came out to meet them. She asked Narayanan, "So, did the wedding go off well?"

Narayanan, who had planned while at Chirukulam to ask her about her welfare and for news of Sangu, was now shy and tongue-tied and could only say "Yes."

Savithri asked, "Gopu, have you seen Appa?"

"No, has he returned?"

"Yes, only yesterday." Savithri lowered her voice. "He has married that girl over there. Her mother, brothers and sisters have also come."

"What of Sangu?" asked Gopalan.

"Nothing is known yet and no further effort has been made to find him since your athimber's return. Appa got the news only after he came back yesterday. It seems your telegram and letter never reached him."

"But I sent them to Vanjanur," said Gopalan.

"I'll tell you all about it later," said Savithri. "The fact is, he knew nothing till last night. I told him as soon as he returned. He said, If that donkey chooses to run away, let him. He'll return of his own accord. I can't be bothered. Now it's only ... he mentioned your athimber by name ... who can go in search again."

Gopalan was so worried and confused by the situation at home that he quite forgot to tell Savithri about his success in the examination. That night, while a tired Narayanan was sound asleep, Savithri called Gopalan to her room and told him of the talk in the village about the Vanjanur wedding. Then she took out a letter and gave it to him saying, "Gopu, you are younger than me, but you're my main support. I have no one else to turn to. There's no point in saying your athimber should be different. It's my karma that he is what he is. This letter came a few days ago when your athimber was away. I thought it was either from you or Sangu, and opened it eagerly. But on reading it, I was completely shocked. You can't imagine the agony I've been undergoing. I'm hardly able to eat or sleep. I've come to think that the only course left for me is to put an end to my life. I've been counting the hours for your return," she wept as she spoke.

The letter was addressed as, "To be given in the hands of Sowbagyavathi Savithri at the home of Sri Seshier in Ariyur," and bore the postmark of Pichiyur, a nearby village. The letter ran thus,

To Savithri, the anchor of my life,

You may be aware that I've been pining for you, captivated by your beauty. Can you blame the moth for being attracted to the flame or the bee for seeking the honey in the flower or iron for being drawn to a magnet? Similarly, you can't blame me for being drawn by your loveliness. It's surely against divine order that you should waste your loveliness on a short darkie. God endows us with beauty only so that we may enjoy life. You needn't worry about people coming to know. Within the next ten days, some evening, according to your convenience, at around six, plant a pumpkin flower on the wall of your backyard. I'll take that as your assent and get prepared. Your husband doesn't sleep at home. He spends his nights with that Marava woman, Sudali. Your father and brothers are now away. At around eleven at night, cover yourself fully with a white cloth and come out. I shall be waiting for you. We can go to the school building standing alone in the north of the town, indulge in pleasure to our hearts' content and return without anyone being the wiser. We can also make suitable plans for the future. Even if your father should return, he would go away to his bungalow. Your brother sleeps upstairs. As for that shaven widow who is with you, she can hardly see even in broad daylight. So, this can certainly be done without anyone's knowledge. If you don't grant your gracious consent, I'll certainly kill myself, and the burden of that death will weigh on you. If perhaps you are not aware of my identity, you'll know soon enough. I may not be quite a match for your beauty, but you certainly cannot find a more handsome man than me hereabouts. Once you know me, you'll never regret your action. Remember that we have to seize every opportunity for pleasure and not waste precious time. Love not enjoyed at the appropriate time is a waste.

Seeking the gift of life from you.

Lovelorn

Gopalan was enraged as he read the letter. Had he known the identity of the writer, he would have gone out immediately and murdered him. He controlled his feelings and pacified Savithri. He then woke up Narayanan and showed him the letter.

Realizing the time was opportune Narayanan told him of how his suspicions had been roused and asserted Nagamier was the one who had written the letter. He got Savithri's books and showed Gopalan the markings to convince him. He had considerable difficulty calming down Gopalan. They put their heads together and hatched a plan. They said nothing to Savithri. Nobody else knew anything of their intentions.

No one in the house noticed the pumpkin flower stuck in a lump of dung on the backyard wall the next evening. That night, at around eleven, when all was quiet, a figure draped in white from top to toe emerged slowly from Seshier's house. As it stepped into the street, a man seated on the thinnai next door with his head covered got up and signalling the first figure to follow him walked briskly northwards glancing behind frequently. When he (that is, Nagamier) reached the veranda of the school, he said to the other figure as it approached, "My darling life! Oh, how lucky I am! What great good fortune!" and caught the figure in an embrace. He knew nothing thereafter. His wretched mouth was gagged with husk-filled rags. Four or five Maravas came running from behind the building, like Yama's messengers. They quickly blindfolded Nagamier and tied him to a pillar. One of them ordered, "Let the puja begin," upon which a bucket of dirty dung water kept ready was poured over Nagamier's head. Another applied a broomstick to his body to dry him. A garland of prickly weeds was thrown round his neck and his tuft was cut off. One of the men simulated the deeparadhanai with a lighted match, singeing Nagamier's moustache. Even before this ceremony had begun, the figure that had followed Nagamier, which was none other than Narayanan, returned home to gleefully report to Gopalan and laugh over it for the rest of the night.

We hesitate to record the other honours bestowed on Nagamier. As a final flourish, he was branded on the thigh by one of the men with the pronouncement, "This is how the pumpkin flowers." Another warned that they were letting him off easily in deference to the master's wishes, and that he should be extremely careful in future. He was then freed and the men left, each spitting on his face. Nagamier tottered to the water tank, bathed and returned home quietly before dawn.

As Gopalan was speechless, Shala put an arm on his shoulder saying, "Someone may come here. Let's go upstairs."

S avithri did not know the identity of the author of the letter. Neither did she see any connection between that letter and the village gossip about Nagamier having lost his tuft while trying to scale a wall. Nagamier kept to his house for a week, saying he was ill with fever. When he emerged, he said his hair had to be cut as it had matted and a short haircut at neck level was the fashion in Madras and other cities. As for the absence of his moustache, he explained he had it removed as it tended to get sticky while eating sago payasam. But Nagamier burned with deep humiliation, the punishment teaching him no lesson, and leaving him only with a firm resolve to somehow destroy Savithri's chastity, if necessary by force. He decided what he had gone through was all at her behest. He did not tell his wife about the true course of events and, unaware of his designs on Savithri, she continued her friendly interactions as usual. Moreover, a new reason had emerged to strengthen the bond, with the discovery of a very involved and distant connection between Shala and Kamakshi Ammal, Seshier's mother-in-law.

While Gopalan did not tell Savithri the facts, he was anxious to put an end to her friendship with Shala before leaving for Sindhupoonthurai. He consulted Narayanan but they could think of no way of doing this. Finally, a rather wild idea occurred to him which he did not share with Narayanan, wanting to execute it first. It was to make a bold pass at Shala, grab her arm and pull her towards him. He assumed that she would wrench herself free, run away and thereafter avoid visiting his home. He reasoned further that she would be too ashamed to talk about the incident and would offer some lame excuses to Savithri. He realized this would be a base act, but assuaged his conscience with the thought that he was punishing Nagamier, and that even if Nagamier came to know about it, he would assume it was an act of revenge and correct his own behaviour.

By chance, an opportunity arose that very evening. Narayanan was reading upstairs. Seshier and Sundaram Iyer were out. The women of the house were busy in the backyard, leaving the front door closed but not bolted. Gopalan, who wanted a word with Savithri, was coming down the stairs when Shala, who was coming in as usual to get her hair plaited, pushed open the front door and entered, closing it behind her. In the darkness of the passage, she did not notice Gopalan at first and saw him only when both tried to go in. Custom did not permit men and women in the same age group to talk to each other. As they stood hesitating, Gopalan decided to grab the occasion and with a thumping heart approached Shala, caught her by the arm and drew her away from the door. And — horror of horrors — to his utter astonishment, instead of wrenching herself free or recoiling in terror like a serpent spotting a kite, with a coy smile she leaned against him unnerving him. He felt faint as his eyes grew dim and his tongue seemed nailed to his mouth. Shala put an arm on his shoulder, "Someone may come here. Let's go upstairs."

This loosened Gopalan's tongue slightly and he said, "Nanu is upstairs."

"Then why do you call me now?" asked Shala. "We'll have to wait. Don't forget, though. There, I can hear someone. I'll have to go." She then kissed Gopalan on both cheeks and hurried in. Gopalan stood rooted to the spot, he did not know for how long, coming to life only when he heard Narayanan call out to him. He then went up the stairs slowly. One look at his face and Narayanan was very concerned. "Why, Gopu? Is anything wrong? Any news about your wife? Or Sangu?"

"No, it's nothing. Don't worry. I'll tell you presently."

When he heard Gopalan's account, Narayanan laughed uproariously. "Pardon me!" he said. "What a pity! I've spoilt things for you like the proverbial bear let loose at puja!"

Gopalan was both angry and scared. "Stop it, Nanu, don't be silly! I'm even more worried now. So far we feared Nagamier, but his wife seems even more dangerous. Savithri should have nothing to do with such people. Do you remember the lecture of our teacher, Subramanya Iyer, at the Youth Association on the tenets of a good domestic life? He quoted Tennyson on the dangers of allowing an unfaithful wife to continue living in one's home, as she would then spread the contagion of her designs further and ruin susceptible men. But the poet was thinking only of the influence of such women on other men. He did not consider the possibility of their leading other women astray. It doesn't matter if Savithri remains an illiterate idiot. She shouldn't associate with Shala, even for the sake of education. What do we do?"

Narayanan thought for a while. "No specific strategy will work. Speak to Savithri. Tell her, that no one seems to have a good word about Shala, that you feel her appearance and behaviour are too coquettish and that she should give up the association. She'll heed your advice and won't question you. If she does, tell her your father too isn't happy about Shala visiting your house. She won't question you further and your objective will be achieved."

Gopalan followed this advice and spoke to Savithri. A couple of days later, the two left for Sindhupoonthurai. Gopalan asked Savithri to write to him when necessary and got her some notepaper and postal envelopes.

Narayanan and Gopalan took to their studies seriously and worked diligently.

Narayanan and Gopalan took to their studies seriously and worked diligently. They also shared a deep love for Tamil, and to learn more of its literature, went every evening to the neighbouring village of Mayanur, to study classics like *Thirukkural*, Thevaram and *Kamba Ramayanam* with a vidwan who was the pujari of a temple. This was a very beneficial association as the man was exceptional in many ways. Older than them, he was learned not only in Tamil but in English, Sanskrit, Telugu and Hindustani as well. Though quite knowledgeable about the ways of the world, he never sought worldly advancement and was only intent on helping others. Any person of any age group would have found the friendship of this good, kind gentleman valuable. For the two friends, he was like an elder brother, giving them advice and guidance and instilling in them proper values. An example follows.

The two young men had studied an English play, in which the poet expressed his views on the qualities of music, and of the untrustworthy nature of the man who could not appreciate music. Narayanan, who was crazy about music and attended many music performances, including those in private homes where he was not invited, wanted to discuss this topic with the Tamil vidwan. To Gopalan however music was only so much noise. The pujari not only had greater love for music and more musical knowledge than Narayanan, but he had also learned to play some instruments.

They were studying *Jeevaka Chintamani*, the ninth century Tamil classic by a Jain poet, and had come to a passage on music.

Narayanan said, "Gopu, Thanjavur Ramamani, a thevadiyal, will be giving a performance at the Tirunelveli temple tomorrow evening. She is considered a wonderful musician. Would you like to go?"

To the pujari's query about the performer, Narayanan elaborated, "She is indeed great. They say that even Maha Vaidyanatha Iyer, the well known exponent of Carnatic music cannot sing the Kalyani raga as well as she does. It's a pity you don't leave the temple premises. I'd be so happy if you could accompany me."

"Not that I'm very strict about it," said the pujari. "But the question is, of all things, do I have to go out for a devadasi's performance?"

"Why do you say so?" asked Narayanan. "How does it matter who performs? We look only to quality. How can the music be sullied by the character of the performer? Does the money got by selling a dog bark?"

"You're right to some extent," admitted the pujari. "But for us, to extend this logic to all our activities is neither possible nor desirable. It is true that a dasi's music by itself is not bad. But if the performance is of a kula magal, it would certainly be superior, even if her chastity does not in any way add to the quality of her music. Let us consider the example of milk in two receptacles – a dirty, smoke stained mud pot and a golden goblet. Both contain the same milk. But by drinking from the mud pot one's lips could get dirty and one might also swallow some impurities. There's no such risk with the golden goblet. Listening to the performance of a virtuous woman, we would only appreciate her talent and consider her husband and parents lucky. No lewd thoughts would cross our mind. But a thevadiyal, while singing, would engage in suggestive smiles, gestures and glances. She would sing padams imparting nuances, and use voice modulations to sound seductive. She would employ all the tricks known to her to make money, not just by singing but by ensnaring men. The mind of man is complex and crafty, and no task is more difficult than bringing it under control. The great self-realized poets, Thayumanavar and

Pattinathupillaiar, have spoken about the dangers women's charms hold for those seeking to control their mind. Of the three desires that possess men – power, wealth and women – the last is the most difficult to resist and overcome. You may recall the verse in *Kamba Ramayanam* where Sage Vasishta advises Rama to beware of the dangers that follow lust for women, comparing the influence that women have on men to the evil effects of a comet on earth. You don't have to take this literally, but certainly infatuation does grow very quickly to an all-consuming obsession. Legend and mythology abound with examples of those who have renounced the world falling victims to the wiles of women."

"What you've said is no doubt true," Narayanan responded. "But I would like you to clarify some of my doubts. Isn't it the duty of all men to cultivate the talents they are endowed with? If we don't cultivate sangitha gnanam, would we not be losing something divine, something gifted by Providence to improve our lives?"

"You're very right, I agree with you. Sangitha gnanam is indeed no ordinary gift. Music is something uniquely wonderful, which can make us forget our worldly worries, capable even of taming wild animals and helping humans to overcome some diseases. At the same time, it is a strong inducer of lust. These are its strong positive and negative aspects. To sustain its glory, music has to be carefully nurtured through good and proper means. Those who revel in the performances of women of easy virtue and consider them the finest exponents aren't rendering a true service to the art. We can surely enjoy music by listening to the performances of chaste kula sthris. We can ourselves learn to sing or play instruments. Today, unfortunately, the glory of music is dimmed because it is largely the preserve of dasis and loose men. I don't mean to say that one should never listen to a dasi's music or that those who do so are invariably ensnared. All I'm trying to say is that if those with a taste for music seek to cultivate it through listening to the performances of dasis, they will, in course of time, lose the aversion all good men should have for such women. This may not drive them into the arms of prostitutes but will certainly break their defences and endanger their character. Rather than run this risk, one should give up music altogether."

Gopalan, who was listening patiently said, "I agree, but I don't understand what is there in music to charm men into losing their senses."

To this Narayanan responded, "Ada, poda! Talking about music to you is like describing the beauty of the Kutralam waterfalls to the blind. You are tone deaf – the sound of the veena and the beat of the town drum are one and the same to you."

They then took leave of the pujari and returned to Sindhupoonthurai. For the record, it has to be noted that Narayanan did not stay away from the music performance at Tirunelveli that night.

While thus improving his Tamil learning, Narayanan was also teaching Padmavati. She had come to Sindhupoonthurai only because he wanted to continue with her education. She studied eagerly and acquired considerable proficiency in Tamil and was able, on her own, to compose verses in folk style. At Narayanan's insistence, she ignored custom and moved freely with Gopalan, addressing him as Anna. Thus she had two teachers, and began to learn English. Apart from this, Narayanan wrote down the words of some good songs sung in the concerts he attended and tried to teach them to Padmavati. And she began to gain some proficiency in music as well.

At times Kamakshi Ammal's harsh taunts pierced her like an arrow and brought unbidden tears.

Seshier's wife Kamalambal came of age within a month of her arrival at her husband's house. The rutu santhi was performed on an auspicious day the following week. Seshier did not invite any relations or even send for Gopalan. His son-in-law Sundaram Iyer was also away, in search of Sangu. The function was attended only by Ayyasami vathiar and the newly discovered relation on his wife's side, Nagamier, who had cultivated familiarity ever since the relationship was revealed. His wife Shala surmised that Savithri's coolness was because of Gopalan's report about her. Smarting from the insult, she conspired against Savithri, aided by Kamakshi Ammal and Kamalambal. In consequence, her visits and association increased, despite the break with Savithri. Savithri herself never visited any home, as her husband did not like it. But Kamakshi Ammal and Kamalambal went over to Shala's house when she was not visiting them and all three continued their gossip about Savithri.

Savithri's agony and mental stress increased day by day. Even after three months, her husband had not returned from his search. Neither was there any letter from him. It was rumoured that he was living comfortably with an acchi in Kerala. When Savithri tried to speak to her father about her worry, he was irritated and said, "He went in search of Sangu. Who is to go in search of him? He's not a child. He'll return of his own accord. What else do you think can be done?"

No longer did Seshier treat his only daughter with his old tenderness and concern. Kamalambal's Curtain Lectures had their effect and he began resenting his children. Earlier, he used to miss his sons so much that a carriage was despatched to fetch them almost every weekend. Now, even during holidays, he sent word to Gopalan to stay on in

Sindhupoonthurai and concentrate on his studies. He wasted no thoughts on Sangu. And it seemed as if he was happy at the disappearance of his son-in-law. Savithri understood all this. She was very unhappy and at night wept bitterly, as her pride would not permit any public display of grief. Her face reflected her depression as she went about her tasks listlessly. At times, Kamakshi Ammal's harsh taunts pierced her like an arrow and brought unbidden tears. She then sought some corner to shed them in private and compose herself. She lost her lustre and became a shadow of her old self. She had no one to turn to, no one from whom she could seek some relief. No one was allowed into the house without Kamakshi Ammal's permission. She even lost interest in her studies. To add to all this, Nagamier was now moving about the house freely, coming right up to the kitchen, staring boldly at Savithri, cheekily responding to the remarks she made to others. In a very short time, he won over both Seshier's wife and mother-in-law. As the saying goes, Is it possible to place a lid on the town's mouth? People began to talk openly, with sarcastic glee about Seshier's matrimonial exploits, that he first spent thousands to get a wife for Cuddalore Vakil Annasami Iyer and, after gathering funds and spending lavishly, had acquired, nurtured and placed in his own home, two wives for Nagamier. Such loose talk spread rapidly and reached Savithri's ears, causing her to shrink with mortification and sorrow. Her plight was like that of Sita when she languished as Ravana's prisoner surrounded by the rakshasis. Even Sita, in an alien land, found a friend amongst them in Thrijada. But Savithri, though in her father's home, had no one. In utter despair, she contemplated suicide and twice went upstairs to hang herself, but somehow lacked the courage. Finally, she wrote the following letter to Gopalan and eagerly awaited his reply.

Ariyur, Tuesday

To my dear brother Gopu,

You will surely not be able to stand the suffering I'm undergoing, were you here to witness it. There are many things I cannot write about. Nagamier and Shala are always in our house. From his behaviour, I've begun to suspect he was the one who wrote that letter. Your athimber has gone away, leaving me in the lurch. Were he here, I'd have left and somehow made a living, seeking an ootuporai or husking grain. You're my only means of deliverance. Appa doesn't care any more. I have no one else. I've thought of a way out. You must act accordingly. It seems your wife is all right now. Take her to Sindhupoonthurai and set up house with her. I will come and stay with you to keep her company. I can put up with any ill treatment from you both, if you're so inclined. Anything would be better than my present predicament. I'm not able to tolerate all that is said and done by these wretched dogs and demons that came in just yesterday. I tried twice to end my life, but could not bring myself to do so. How can I? I still have to live out my destiny and suffer the many tribulations in store, wedded as I am to your athimber. If you don't make some arrangement by Sunday, I'll surely end my life somehow or the other and you'll not see me again. Don't worry about the expenses. With all of us out of the house, Appa will be happy to give us some money. If not, you can ask for help from your father-in-law. If that too fails, there's my jewellery, which can sustain us, even if it takes you thirty years to start earning. If you have the slightest sympathy for me and wish to see me alive, please start preparations and come.

Your affectionate sister,

Savithri

The four days that followed the despatch of this letter seemed like four yugas to Savithri. On Saturday night, in response to Gopalan's letter, his brother-in-law arrived with Kalyani. And Gopalan himself came the next morning. Seshier's conscience began to trouble him when Gopalan said he wished to take Kalyani and Savithri with him to Sindhupoonthurai and his face reflected something of his old love and concern for his children. But he raised no objection. He gave Gopalan fifty rupees cash as well as a letter for his secretary in Tirunelveli, directing the latter to make a regular monthly allowance. When they left, he hesitantly followed their cart a long distance, much like a milch cow following her calf. He did not speak to his wife or his mother-in-law that day. However, the affection he felt for his children and the anger against his wife were transient, like summer lightning.

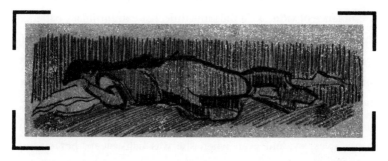

She drowned both herself and him in misery through her tantrums. Even contrite apologies from him failed to soothe her.

Savithri, Kalyani and Padmavati moved with true affection, understanding and oneness, like sisters born to the same mother, reared with love and married to men of means and education. This harmonious association, like three swans in a pond, brought much happiness to all. At the same time, there were many differences in their nature and intelligence as in their looks.

We have earlier described Savithri's beauty and character. The humiliation she had to suffer on account of her husband and her mounting troubles checked her vivacity and gave her natural liveliness a semblance of sadness. At the same time, her extraordinary patience and understanding made her wise beyond her years. Her seniority in age, greater maturity and the celibate life she was leading, automatically made her assume the role of the eldest sister, guiding and counselling the other two.

Kalyani was very fair and slim. There was extraordinary beauty in her eyes, evident even when she was half-asleep, her eyelids partially closed. Gopalan would often sit by her side as she slept, lost in this loveliness. Loving and lovable, she became the centre of her husband's existence but ... there was a source of tension. This lay in her temperament. She was very stubborn and wilful. The youngest daughter of rich and doting parents, she had been thoroughly spoilt, allowed to have her way in everything. Any attempt to check or correct caused a temper tantrum. Criticism by someone she loved resulted in a torrent of tears followed by the accusation that it was a deliberate attempt to hurt her. Gopalan came to know this side of her nature right at the outset. When her wish was crossed on some trivial matter, Kalyani accused him of being heartless and without any love for her. She drowned both herself and him in misery through her tantrums. Even contrite apologies from him failed to soothe her. On such occasions, Gopalan was in a quandary. What was he to do when his beloved wife sobbed and her beautiful eyes streamed? He could not understand how she, who could transport him to divine levels of bliss, could also torture herself and him for the most trifling of reasons. He even began to wonder if this was a recurrence of her old trouble, attributed to the influence of supernatural powers. All he could do was to indulge her and give in even on important matters, ignoring the harm this might cause in the long run. He also advised Savithri to deal with her carefully. His only objective was to avoid the torrent of tears. Kalyani's temperament was like the monsoon sky, clear and sunny one moment, and covered with clouds and rife with lightning the next.

Padmavati, still a child, was growing up fast. She was by nature the most playful of the three, but one feature of her character outweighed this. She always aimed to please her husband, to follow his inclinations and ensure his love and devotion. This unwavering prime quest of hers was reflected in all her actions – she was not worried about her bodily discomforts, about eating or sleeping, about insult or injury. She always anticipated his wishes and acted accordingly. If she studied hard, it was because she knew Narayanan wanted this above all else. Because he had appreciated the way she had dressed one day, she took pains to follow that style. Fresh and neat, she sat down every evening to sing, so that her husband would be pleased when he returned from school. If her life could be compared to a pearl necklace, her sole intent of pleasing her husband was the silken thread which strung the pearls together, giving shape and support to the necklace.

What would be the answer to the question as to who was the most beautiful of the three, who the best tempered and who the luckiest? Savithri was the best in looks and figure, with the loveliest lips and hair. Kalyani's eyes and grace were the finest. In the cast of limbs, Padmavati was the best. In patience and kindness, Savithri was unrivalled. Kalyani led in love and affection and Padmavati in attention to her husband's wishes and zest. On balance, it would seem that of the three, Padmavati was the luckiest and Savithri the unluckiest. Kalyani was sometimes at the peak of happiness and at others in the depths of despair. Padmavati's good fortune was more stable.

Gopalan had rented the house next to Narayanan's, so that they lived and moved as one family. One evening Savithri was combing and plaiting Kalyani's and Padmavati's hair. Gopalan and Narayanan sat with their books, some distance away. Seethai Ammal, who was like a mother to all of them, had gone to the Siva temple at Kailasapuram for Somavara darshanam.

Narayanan drew Gopalan's attention to an English poem he was reading, which he felt was very apt. He read out a couple of stanzas and Savithri asked him to explain the meaning for their benefit.

Gopalan said, "Meaning? Well, it is all about you people. This was written by an English poet called Pope and his point is that women are so unsteady by temperament that they can only be described by their personal attributes, for instance colour and complexion."

Padmavati said softly to Savithri, yet audibly enough, "What is that? I can't follow what Anna says."

Narayanan took up the explanation. "Men can accomplish things because they are firm in their ideas and pursue their objective steadily, which is beyond women. Of a man, it is possible to say, for instance, that he's short tempered but listens to reason, or that, another is of high integrity and never strays from the truth. One can associate certain characteristics with individual men, which is not possible with women, because they lack that firmness of purpose and strength of mind. So women can only be described by their appearance, that one is short, another fat, yet another tall or that one is dark and the other fair."

Padmavati responded with a laugh. "Take me, for instance. One day I just adore that little calf but at other times, can't stand the sight of it. I'm not steady even in this small matter."

Gopalan laughed and said, "Take another example. If one wants to fix a firm attribute to Padmavati, it can be said that she always acts in line with her husband's wishes. Going by another's wishes is not really an individualistic trait, but since she's consistent in that respect, we can count it as one. But what can we say of Kalyani?" Then smilingly looking at his wife, he continued, "Kalyani, Padmavati acts according to the wishes of another. Shall we say that you want everyone to act according to your wishes, or else burst into tears?"

This was meant as a jocular remark which Gopalan thought would be appreciated by all, particularly Kalyani. But most unexpectedly, the relaxed, playful atmosphere vanished in a trice, as the calm unruffled surface of a pond is disturbed by a pebble. Even as Gopalan was speaking, Kalyani rose and weeping, curled up in a corner. One by one, each of them tried to pacify her, pleading, reassuring, threatening enmity, but nothing had any effect. Gopalan was very angry. He sat by her side, asking forgiveness, expressing distress and cajoling, but Kalyani wept all the more. Finally, in utter disgust, he said, "Pope was cent per cent right," got up, and walked out. Savithri sat by Kalyani's side for a long while and finally managed to quieten her. But Kalyani did not speak normally to anyone that day.

At that time a gypsy came by singing. His song was
very appealing, set in a lively folk tune.

Over a year had passed since the events described in the last chapter. As this was their final year in school, Narayanan and Gopalan were studying hard. Narayanan was no longer so interested in music performances and they stopped reading Tamil with the pujari of Mayanur. Gopalan's aim was to secure a pass in the examination in order to avoid the embarrassment of failure being associated with his wife's presence. As for Narayanan, he wanted above all to complete his studies and begin earning before Padmavati came of age and they started life together. While they both put in a lot of effort, Gopalan suffered from a serious handicap. His wife insisted on his going to bed at nine. If he did not she was angered and upsetting Kalyani was something Gopalan wanted to avoid at all costs. He tried to overcome the difficulty by sometimes getting up and studying after Kalyani had gone to sleep. But the situation caused him much frustration, distress and disgust.

One day, while Narayanan and Gopalan were busy with their books, Savithri sat close by, playing with a little child. It was clear from the child's appearance, his mother's complexion and eyes and his father's wavy hair, that he was born to Gopalan and Kalyani. The child's parentage was further confirmed by the way Savithri fondled him and Gopalan's happy reaction and inward glee. Narayanan was busy at work, unaware of Gopalan's wavering attention and the child's charming antics. Finally, Gopalan said, "Nanu, I think we've studied enough for today. I feel lazy and out of sorts. Let's relax for a while. Just see how this little fellow is playing." Narayanan duly closed his book and the three of them concentrated on the child, finding new meanings in his gestures and prattle. Savithri seemed unusually happy that day, and the old glow had returned to her face after many months. A rare exuberance had replaced her usual calmness.

Gopalan said, "Nanu, don't think my dear sister is so happy because of the antics of her nephew. That's only an excuse. You know there was a letter from Athimber a week ago. It's over a year since he went in search of Sangu. We didn't even know his whereabouts all these days. He has written to say he was in Kerala and would return soon. Someone has now given the information that he's supposed to come today, by the Mail. That is the secret of Savithri's joy."

Savithri was embarrassed but laughed even more, confirming Gopalan's appraisal. Over the months, she had begun to forget her disgust over her husband's lecherous behaviour, and had come to feel she could forgive all and even serve the Marava woman Sudali, the Kerala acchi and all his other mistresses, if only he would return and live with her. She sometimes despaired that this was never to be, that she might perhaps never see him again. She recalled the rare instances of conjugal happiness she had shared with her husband in the seven or eight years of their life together, and completely forgot all the indignities and sorrow she had been subjected to. Indeed, she began to feel she had failed in her duty as a wife. She prayed he should return and resolved that she would do everything possible to make him happy and earn his love. She imagined that hearing of her sufferings while he was away, he would be so moved that he would never part from her again. Until that evening, she was the embodiment of the sorrows of separation. But with the unexpected news of her husband's imminent return, her joy was akin to the emotion that the gift of sight brought to a blind man, or the birth of a child to a woman considered barren, or wealth regained by a man who had suffered its loss. Her mood was infectious and the entire household was lighthearted that day. Narayanan said, "Padmi, come here. We are all in such a good mood. Amma hasn't yet come back from Kailasapuram after darshanam. Do sing for us, don't be shy."

Padmavati began to sing a classical piece, but before she could go on, Gopalan said, "This is too slow, like the Thiruvarur temple chariot. Let's have something light and lively."

Padmavati, after some hesitation, sang a folk song. At that time, a gypsy came by singing. His song was very appealing, philosophical, highlighting the basic uncertainties of life, but set in a lively folk tune. He asked for alms and Padmavati ran in immediately to get some food for him. While the others were talking to the gypsy, Sundaram Iyer entered, a bundle tucked under his arm. He had grown darker and looked like a blacksmith returning home after the day's labour. Savithri could hardly restrain her tears at his appearance. Gopalan was also upset, but Sundaram Iyer himself was oblivious to the reactions. He reported that his search for Sangu had been fruitless and then said, eagerly, "I say, Gopu, Nanu Iyer, do you know that some excellent dramas are being staged at the west temple entrance in Tirunelveli? Tonight, they will be putting up *Harishchandra,* a splendid show, they say. Many bigwigs, zamindars, collectors, vakils, will be there. Why don't we all go?"

Gopalan said, "Not bad, Athimber! We live here but are not aware of this! You're better informed. What do you say, Nanu? Our evening study schedule is upset anyway and so we might drop the night's as well. But Athimber, wouldn't you like to rest? You must be tired after your journey. We can go to the play tomorrow, it'll certainly be on, it is not going to run away."

"Oh no, I'm not tired," insisted Sundaram Iyer. "They say tonight's is a particularly good show. I can catch up on my sleep tomorrow."

And so they decided to go after dinner. Savithri was bitterly disappointed that her husband, returning after more than a year, did not exchange even a word with her, but sought the pleasure of entertainment immediately after stepping into the house. She went in with streaming eyes, the joy that had suffused her vanishing like the moon under total eclipse.

Nanu, where is he? Where is Gopu's Athimber?

The fire that destroyed the Narasingha Rayar drama tent at the west entrance of Tirunelveli temple on the night of Monday, the twelfth of Aani and the loss of life it caused are widely known. Those who witnessed the disaster and its aftermath in the early hours of Tuesday still shudder at the recollection. We do not have the heart to describe this in detail and shall only take account of what is relevant to our story.

> But what a tragic waste it was!
> Our hearts grieve for those lost lives,
> The only sons of mothers, youths yet to taste life,
> Newly wedded grooms, men at fatherhood's threshold,
> And yet others, fathers already,
> The solace of their embraces now denied to their children,
> So many, all, all lost in the relentless flames.

They were already restless that those who had gone to Tirunelveli had not returned. The news of the fire spread rapidly to Sindhupoonthurai and adjoining areas. The agitation in the homes of Narayanan and Gopalan defies description. There was no man around who could be despatched to get news. And they did not have the courage to ask an outsider. Their wailing and weeping moved a neighbour to offer to go to Tirunelveli. He tried to reassure them advising them to have faith in god and left. After dawn, Seethai Ammal also left.

It is not right to dwell on tragic events. That afternoon, at around two, Seethai Ammal returned with Narayanan in a carriage and Gopalan in a palanquin, lain on tender banana leaves. Gopalan was unconscious. Narayanan had some slight burns on the back and the shoulder, sustained while trying to save Gopalan. Seeing her husband covered with burns, unrecognizable and wavering between life and death, Kalyani swooned and required attention in the midst of all the commotion. Savithri stood still for a long while, tears streaming down her eyes. Then she suddenly collected herself and asked "Nanu, where is he? Where is Gopu's Athimber?"

Narayanan turned his tear-stained face away without replying. The shock that struck Savithri was like a bolt of lightning. Wringing her hands, she said "Ayyo, ada paavi, tell me, tell me what happened?" and then ran inside to Seethai Ammal crying, "Amma, can't you at least tell me? What happened to my husband? Tell me Amma, where is my husband?"

When Seethai Ammal replied, "Adiyamma Savithri, what can I say? The wretched gods have betrayed you. Why should this fate visit you?" Savithri sank to the ground, senseless. It was only after some time that she began to sob and gave way to tears. Her sorrow was too deep for description. Perhaps Kamban's picture of Sita, held captive in Asokavana by Ravana, could bear comparison: Sita, overcome with the utter despair of helplessness, sobbed, swooned, prayed to the Lord, her agony precluding all other sensations.

When he heard the news of the fire on Tuesday morning, Seshier immediately left for Tirunelveli to ensure that all was well with his son. He learnt of the events first hand. He sent Gopalan with Seethai Ammal and then, together with some pallbearer brahmins, searched for the charred body of his son-in-law and identified it through some jewellery worn. He had the body taken to the cremation ground, performed the last rites, and came to Sindhupoonthurai. He was completely shattered. One of his sons was considered lost, the other was battling for life and his dear daughter was widowed.

He gave way to his grief, repeatedly beating his face and banging his head on the wall.

Only time is the ultimate healer. Once the initial shock and grief subside a little, the survivors do begin to think of whatever is in their interest. Seshier realized immediate action was necessary to save Gopalan. Moving him to Ariyur was out of question. It would be utterly foolish, since, apart from a barber there was no medical facility in that village, while modern treatment from a qualified doctor was available in Palayamkottai. Narayanan's uncle and Gopalan's father-in-law also arrived to see their sons-in-law. The Palayamkottai doctor called twice a day. He didn't offer much hope at first. But thanks to the strength of Kalyani's mangalyam, Gopalan's condition showed improvement. They gave him constant and total attention, day and night, following the doctor's instructions religiously.

In an earlier chapter, we had occasion to speak of the teaching profession, hailing it as the noblest of all callings. We must admit that we had not then considered the nobility of the medical profession. For advancement in learning, culture and wisdom, a healthy constitution is essential. Those born on this earth must die some day, but so long as there is life, good health is all important. The doctor who devotes his life to promoting this is certainly the most munificent of men. If our life on this earth is compared to a kingdom, the physician would be the commander-in-chief warring ceaselessly against Yama. He actually is our Brahma incarnate. In our anxiety, we consider him as one capable of conquering fate. When his face reflects hope, we are steeped in joy. But when he appears even slightly worried we sink in an ocean of despair. There are many who revel in self-satisfaction after rendering some small help to another. But what of the doctor who saves lives? Is his sense of satisfaction measurable? If he takes pride in his achievements, it is justified and cannot be considered egoistic. No career is nobler than his.

With the gentle and patient care of the great man, Narayanan was able to go to school within a week while Gopalan improved steadily and crossed the critical stage. The fee of one thousand rupees paid by Gopalan's father cannot certainly be considered too much for the services rendered.

Without any one's knowledge, she quietly took Kalyani's large mirror to a room. A sharp cry Amma! followed.

In accordance with the dictates of custom and caste, Savithri was disfigured. Unable to bear the thought of witnessing it, Narayanan went away to Mayanur that day. Even the barber, called upon to shave her lovely locks, was deeply affected. There was constant weeping in the house and no one could force down a morsel that day. Kalyani and Padmavati felt more fear than grief. The thought that only a hair's breadth of luck had saved them from a similar fate left them rigid. As for Savithri, she appeared the embodiment of the tragedy of young widowhood. A strange thought crossed her mind that evening and soon became an obsession. She never spent time preening or taking pride in her looks, using a mirror only while applying the pottu. And when someone else did that and asked her to consider the effect in a mirror, she would merely shrug and say, "Oh, this will do very well for me," and spurn the mirror. And this Savithri now had an uncontrollable urge to look at her reflection. Without any one's knowledge, she quietly took Kalyani's large mirror to a room. A sharp cry, Amma! followed. Seethai Ammal rushed in to find the mirror shattered and Savithri senseless on the floor. She was revived with difficulty.

Savithri suffered intense torment. While at times she thought it would have been better had her husband remained in Kerala for the rest of his life, at others she wished she had succeeded in her suicide attempts and predeceased him. She felt had she been widowed while still a young, innocent girl, the pain would have been less. There were times when she wished she had never been born, blaming herself for not preventing her husband from going to the play. She also felt she should have insisted on going along with him, as some women had done. She blamed the gods often and the drama troupe sometimes. At times, she sobbed loudly and at others she sat still with red, swollen eyes, lifeless like a portrait. Very often, she contemplated suicide. Sometimes, very rarely though, she forgot herself watching Gopalan's child, but sudden recollection of the past followed soon, increasing her sorrow and ending in choking sobs.

In course of time the intensity of her grief lessened. Her love for the little child, for the brother she had nearly lost, and for the father who was steeped in sorrow over her fate, started taking its place. Gopalan and Narayanan thought of ways and means to distract her, through Gopalan's child and through involving her in literary and philosophical readings and discussions. Attending on Gopalan in the first two months, giving him medicines and feeding him, was also something that employed her mind and helped distract her. Seshier wanted to take them all to Ariyur for a change, but none of them cared for that and it was decided they would go only after Gopalan's examinations. After Gopalan started going to school again, Seshier left for Ariyur.

Narayanan had only two or three scars on his body but, as can be imagined, Gopalan was badly disfigured. This caused him much distress.

People made all sorts of loose remarks about the child's features. But Seshier was devoted to the child.

There were a number of developments in Ariyur since we were there last. In the first place, Nagamier had perished in the Tirunelveli fire. He had gone to the play with a mistress. Some survivors of the disaster reported that he had tried to escape by climbing the temple tower but his mistress had pulled him down, crying that she was not to be left behind. He had fallen down and broken his leg and both of them had been burnt. After his death, one of his brothers-in-law had come and taken Shala to Kumbakonam, their hometown.

A baby girl was born to Kamalambal, Seshier's wife. People made all sorts of loose remarks about the child's features and resemblances. But Seshier was devoted to the child, the first girl in the family after Savithri. She was dear also to Savithri and Gopalan who had arrived after the examinations. However, Kamakshi Ammal would not permit any one other than herself and her daughter to even touch the baby. Now that Seshier had started to show some renewed affection for his children, he too was prohibited from fondling the child. Any one approaching her was told sharply, "Let her be, she's a pauper after all." Kamakshi Ammal would then point to Gopalan's son and say, "Over there is the heir apparent, make much of him." Kalyani could not bear the taunts and insults of Kamakshi Ammal and Kamalambal and was always on the verge of tears. Savithri seemed indifferent, moving about in a daze and trying to keep peace by taking on all the household tasks. The atmosphere made Gopalan spend all his time upstairs, coming down only for meals. He was eagerly awaiting the examination results. He had made up his mind to continue his studies in Madras, in case he passed, or to return to Sindhupoonthurai, in case he failed. In any event, he was determined to take Kalyani and Savithri with him. Savithri was equally firm about going away with him, regardless of what people said and what tradition demanded. She could not bear the mere thought of continuing under Kamakshi Ammal's authority.

Narayanan made a sudden appearance one day. He brought good news. The results of the examination were known. He had passed in the first division and Gopalan in the second. He had come, he said, to give this news and to consult Gopalan on some matters. Gopalan, Savithri and Kalyani were happier at the prospect of leaving Ariyur than over the examination result.

That evening, Narayanan and Gopalan sat upstairs and had a heart to heart talk. Narayanan explained that though he was extremely keen on continuing his studies, it seemed circumstances might not permit it. While it was not imperative that he should start earning, his uncle's financial position was not strong enough to support his higher education. His uncle's debts were increasing. His wife would never allow further expenditure on Narayanan's education. Seethai Ammal was stubborn about following her son to Madras, should he decide to go there. And Narayanan wanted Padmavati to accompany them, so that her studies could continue. Since Narayanan was the only one to secure a first class in their district, he would be eligible for a scholarship from the Madras Christian College, which would include waiver of college fees and a cash payment of not less than seven rupees per month. Narayanan could expect a further ten rupees from his uncle. He was desperately keen on snatching at this opportunity but could not see how three persons could live on seventeen rupees per month in Madras, where house rent alone would eat up at least five or six rupees, and where everything, including firewood, was sold by weight. The option of employment was available and he could earn ten to fifteen rupees per month, but Narayanan did not have the heart to consider this, keen as he was on continuing his studies.

"Don't worry, Nanu!" Gopalan responded. "Savithri and I have already discussed this. You don't have to pay any fees. You can use my books. If you come to Madras alone, you can stay with us and need not incur any household expenditure at all. Even if Amma and Padmavati accompany you, there's nothing to worry about. I'm going to rent a large house. All of us can stay in it. You don't have to worry about rent. Don't feel that seventeen rupees will not do for the three of you. How can we be separated? Even in this short time, I've missed you badly. If you give up your studies now, I'll have to follow suit. I can't go to Madras and study on my own without you. You should not be formal, if you're a true friend."

Gopalan was very persuasive. Finally they decided to proceed to Madras. After consulting Seshier, a date for the journey was also fixed. Narayanan left for Chirukulam to get ready and to meet Gopalan at Sindhupoonthurai on an agreed date along with his mother and wife. We can now meet our friends again only in Chennaipuri.

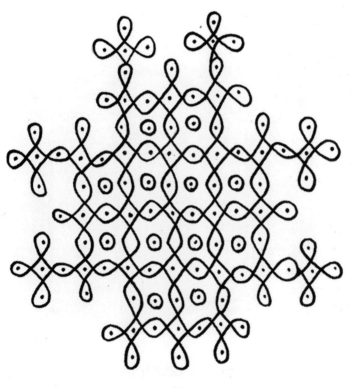

PART II

Spurning material advancement, he crossed the seas to become a professor.

F or those with an intuitive understanding of the Supreme Being who permeates this universe, no explanation of His qualities is necessary, while for those without such understanding, no explanation is possible – so one of my teachers used to remark. This dictum could apply with equal force in respect of the wonders and strange sights of Chennaipuri. However, since movement has been greatly facilitated through the vast spread of the railways throughout Tamil Nadu, most citizens would have visited the capital of the Presidency and seen these for themselves. Hence, it would be appropriate to limit descriptions of the city to such situations as required in the story.

On reaching Madras, our friends Narayanan and Gopalan stayed at the home of a friend in Triplicane. They were accompanied only by Seethai Ammal, Savithri and Kalyani. Despite Narayanan's best efforts, Padmavati did not come with them. Ayyavier would not consider sending her so far away when she was approaching puberty. Though greatly disappointed at this abrupt end to Padmi's education, Narayanan had to accept the situation out of deference to the wishes of elders and fear of that great bugbear, Custom.

On arrival, the two friends were mainly concerned with choosing a college. Gopalan preferred the Government Presidency College. But Narayanan had appeared for the examination to qualify for a scholarship at the Christian College. The prospect of separation from him made Gopalan decide on the same college. As educational institutions had already opened, the two friends set out to have a look at the college of their choice the day after their arrival. As they reached Triplicane High Road, their ears were assailed by the din of jutka drivers calling out for passengers. Cries such as "One for

Mannadi," "For Mylapore, one-one," "Pookadai ekadmi," "Come on saar, come," rent the air. They were confused at first, not understanding what it was all about. Then, steadying themselves, they signalled to a jutka driver. He responded with such alacrity that it seemed his vehicle would knock them down. They hurriedly moved aside, and told him they wanted to go to the Christian College. He did not understand at first, but after listening intently, said, "Oh, Miller School?" This remark removed the tinge of regret in Gopalan's mind about forgoing Presidency College. Ignorant of the prevailing hire charges, they decided it would be best to offer the jutka driver half of what he demanded. Starting with four annas, they finally settled for six annas. When they got into the carriage, the horse moved backwards at a brisk pace to the vast amusement of the other jutka drivers. Gopalan and Narayanan's embarrassment soon changed to alarm at the prospect of ending up in the gutter. The cartman's attempts to cajole the horse to correcting its course were loftily ignored by the animal. But when he resorted to the cane, it began to run forward at full speed. Scared further by the rattling of the whip on the wheel, the horse proceeded as if in a frenzy. When finally deposited at Christian College, the two friends, badly shaken, had to cope further with the loud insistence of the jutka driver that they had actually agreed to a fare of eight annas. Too scared to argue, they paid up and entered the college.

The Madras Christian College is a towering structure, three stories high, accommodating the study of a wide range of subjects, from the First Standard to the postgraduate level. It is amongst the foremost colleges in this country in respect of student strength and quality of instruction. The innumerable classrooms are always filled with the sound of instruction and the response of students. As far as South

India is concerned, it is without doubt the best institution. It has been established and is run by padres who have come to this country from Scotland to spread Christianity. Their guiding principle is that with the spread of education and the development of the mind, true faith would automatically establish itself. Most of the European teachers in the college are padres. Every day, all classes begin with a prayer and a reading from the Bible. The study of the Bible is also set as a special subject, and prizes are instituted for students excelling in it. However, the number of students converting to Christianity on this account is negligible.

The teachers of this college, like other Europeans in India, spend the greater part of their lives far from home, under difficult climatic conditions. But unlike the Europeans teaching in other educational institutions, they do not receive salaries commensurate with their effort, but are paid only what is strictly necessary for a comfortable life. Even out of this sum, some of them provide assistance to poor students. Their magnanimity appears all the more great when one considers the fact that all this effort is made on behalf of Hindus, Muslims and others who decry the Christian religion. There is little doubt that students who receive instruction from such men and have the opportunity to associate with them gain a new perspective, growing less selfish and more keen on helping others.

Narayanan and Gopalan were awestruck by the crowd of students and the sheer size of the institution. They sought the room of the principal, Dr Miller. At that time the great scholar was about fifty years old. He had an imposing personality, with a straight and dignified bearing, sharp, piercing eyes beneath bushy eyebrows, a wide forehead lined by his concern for others, and a firm mouth. His presence, gentle and gracious, spontaneously evoked respect and admiration.

Born to wealth and position in Scotland, he achieved academic excellence. Spurning material advancement, he crossed the seas to become a professor in the Christian College. All this was while he was still a youth, at an age when romantic inclinations usually predominate. With his ability and talents, he rose to be the head of the institution which became, to academicians and to the average man, synonymous with his name. He brought in substantial sums from his personal property for the improvement of the institution and the assistance of poor students. He remained a bachelor making the Goddess of Learning his bride, his students his sons, and their care the ruling passion of his life.

Our friends were immediately captivated by his sympathy and understanding. When Narayanan said that he expected to study with the aid of a scholarship, Dr Miller placed his arms around the shoulders of the two as lovingly as a father. Hugging them, and enquiring about their family, he took them to the room where the results of the scholarship examination were available. Learning that Narayanan had passed, he congratulated him warmly. He personally conducted the two to the class they were to join, BA first year, and introduced them to the professor. They both chose History.

In a class examination, Narayanan came out at the top,
scoring eighty per cent, while Gopalan was at the bottom,
with only nine.

Since their college was in the town area, Narayanan and Gopalan felt that living in Triplicane would be inconvenient. They fixed up a house in Ekambareswarar Agraharam and moved into it within a week. Gopalan paid the entire rent of ten rupees. This and his other expenses totalled around fifty rupees per month, for which his father sent a regular remittance, besides instructing a hundi establishment to meet any extra demands from him. Narayanan had no expenses on account of rent and college fees and his other requirements were limited. He received a stipend of seven and a half rupees from the College, and his father-in-law sent him some money as well.

The two friends, who differed much in economic status, started showing marked difference in their scholastic performance as well. Narayanan was fully intent on his studies, and it took up virtually all his time. His mother saw to it that he had no domestic worries, and the separation from Padmi was the only thing that caused him some sadness. When he was overcome by emotion on this account he would, in private, take out the clothes that Padmi had worn on the fourth day of their wedding when, dressed as a boy, she had been taken round the village in a procession. These clothes which he had secretly brought with him, bore the marks of the sandal, turmeric and kumkumam that had adorned her body, and he now clasped them to his bosom, seeking comfort from a vicarious contact. Generally, he spent the mornings in study. In the evenings he would first look through the day's lessons and then go out, either to play football or to walk on the beach with Gopalan. Back home by seven, he would have his dinner and study until ten or eleven, and rising before dawn, again return to his books. With steady interest and commitment to his studies, he quickly gained a reputation for excellence, praised alike by his teachers and fellow students, and indeed was a shining example for the entire institution.

Gopalan, on the other hand, faced many obstacles in the pursuit of his studies. Apart from a brief morning session with Narayanan, he was seldom able to devote any time to his books. In the evenings, while Narayanan worked, Gopalan would be with his wife and child, trying to make up for the hours of separation during the day. Quite often he took his wife to the beach. They were always late getting back, around eight or nine, especially on moonlit nights, and under no circumstance was he allowed to study after nine. An attempt, for any special reason, to snatch an hour's study would mean three days spent in appeasing his darling wife. Study in the morning was hardly possible. Altogether, Gopalan was deeply troubled, the situation at his home in Ariyur, the domestic worries in Madras, the great sorrow on account of Savithri, together with his love for his wife and child, added up to an insurmountable barrier to his scholastic career. As the situation worsened, he was pulled up by his teachers and lost the esteem of his fellow students. He berated himself strongly, and was hurt and unhappy, like an ensnared deer.

In a class examination, Narayanan came out at the top, scoring eighty per cent, while Gopalan was at the bottom, with only nine. Sadness about his friend's humiliation outweighed Narayanan's pleasure at his own success. Gopalan's eyes brimmed with tears while still in class. Their professor used the opportunity to lecture on the difference between diligence and negligence, citing the example of the performances of two friends of the same age and from the same place.

Gopalan's appearance when he came home that evening could be compared to that of Ravana returning after the first day's battle with Rama, as described by Kamban,

He glanced not at his glorious city,
Nor the throngs of friends,
Nor his vast, ocean like army.
While lovely maidens stood still,
Gazing at him surprised,
He had eyes for only one – the Lady Earth.

Gopalan cast his books aside, spoke to no one, and sat sighing deeply, chin in hand. His wife's loving concern and his child's sweet prattle only served to increase the pain, like spears driven into a raw wound. After a while, Narayanan coaxed him to go out with him. On the beach, both were quiet for a long while. Finally, breaking the silence, Narayanan said, "Gopu, I know you said that you hadn't done well. But I thought you would've got at least two out of five right. I never dreamt it would be so bad."

Gopalan said, "I knew right away. I've been neglecting my work, and for the whole week before the exam, I didn't so much as touch my books. Indeed, even the marks I did get were an act of grace."

"But you took your books to the bedroom every night."

"This is very personal. But if I can't talk to you about it, who else can I turn to? True, the books went with me to the bedroom. True too, my eyes reddened with lack of sleep. But as for studies, it was zero – double zero. Kalyanam was indisposed for about a week. She made a great fuss and finally when a small boil, the size of a berry, appeared on her knee, I had to tell her stories long into the night to make her forget the pain. And after she fell asleep, there could be no light in the room."

"But you could've come out and joined me after she was asleep. You knew I was studying until midnight."

"This question wouldn't have occurred to you if you had a wife like mine. I'd certainly have joined you if only I could've got away. Awake or asleep, she'll not let me leave her side. On the very rare occasions she asks me to study, I'm overjoyed. But studies mean nothing to her. If I refuse or contradict her, she's deeply hurt. I just can't stand it when she cries. Listen to the kural verse I've composed about her, Agree and there's no end to the joy she endows, Disagree, and you wear a crown of sorrows."

"What you should do is to interest her in studies and make her read Tamil books while you work. Or ..."

"How can I possibly explain to someone so inexperienced? Our conversation is beginning to sound like the story of the five blind men's encounter with an elephant. If you could possibly hide yourself and watch us one night, you might understand. You know how Savithri Akka started studying. You were yourself the main stimulus for that. And you know the progress she has made. She hasn't taken up English only because she fears such an attempt by a widow would be ridiculed. Otherwise, by now she would've been quite proficient in that language too. She values learning and is very interested and committed. To tell the truth, she spends more time with her books — the Ramayanam, Bhagavatham and Mahabharatam — than I with my texts despite the fact that I'm here primarily to get a college education and am spending over fifty rupees a month on that. Kalyanam is very different. Even the little effort she makes at studies is because I goad her. She's not in the least interested in learning. I've got her the English primer five times, three times here and twice back home, but Kalyanam has not yet proceeded to Lesson Five. They have all been torn up by our Raja. If she reads for a day, she doesn't touch the books for five."

"I still believe this is all your fault," insisted Narayanan. "If she really loves you, would she ignore your wishes and hurt you? You should handle her properly. After all, she's still a child and can be moulded."

"Don't persist in being impractical. Of her love, I have absolutely no doubt. What Hamlet said to Ophelia would perfectly describe her feelings. I had ample evidence of that – her distress when I injured my foot playing ball the other day, and the torments she suffered when I was hovering between life and death with burns from the drama fire. That accident has badly disfigured me, but it hasn't affected her love for me. That, certainly, is no pretence. Actually, if she were only pretending to love me, she would've taken care to placate me. But no, she gets into tearful tantrums for the most trivial reasons. Had you known this, you wouldn't have talked as you did."

"Perhaps closer association with women who are interested in studies might make a difference. Don't you think she might be inclined to study when Padmi comes here?"

"I've no such hope. After all, she has Savithri's example. Do you remember the Tamil verse about how a dog's tail cannot be sharpened to make a writing tool or a burial ground cleaned and lighted to make a home? I don't remember the rest of it. I think she's just not capable of studying. She only weeps and weeps, so much so that I fear her eyes might be affected."

Gopalan went on to recount the happenings of the previous night. He had been telling Kalyani a story. But he was very tired, having walked all the way from Mylapore that evening. He dozed off. Kalyani had had a nap in the afternoon and was wide awake. "She accused me of partiality," said Gopalan. "She said that had I been with Savithri Akka or you or Amma or any of my friends, I would've chatted throughout the night but that with her I always fell asleep even before a conversation began. She started weeping and all my efforts to placate her failed. Finally I was disgusted and decided to sleep. But in a short while her sobbing led to a fit which was quite frightening. So I had to get up and managed to pacify her with great difficulty. But once her good mood was restored, our mutual pleasure knew no bounds. Is any serious study possible in this sort of a situation? Is it not a surprise that I got the marks I did?"

Gopalan grew introspective. "I sometimes wonder whether it is at all worthwhile pursuing studies. After all, I don't have to pass an exam and take up a job. I could go home or to some other place, indulge in the whims of my wife and live happily, enjoying the sort of conjugal bliss that has been praised from time immemorial but is truly rare. But then that seems to me an existence at a base, animal-like level. With a sensible educated wife, it should still be possible to lead such a life, and also make it meaningful and useful to society. But if Kalyanam and I were to start such a life, all ideas of helping others, all interests in good books — indeed in all actions that lend meaning to human existence — would slowly disappear. We would only be indulging in carnal pleasure. You cannot imagine the thoughts that have crossed my mind. I've contemplated suicide, I have thought of murdering Kalyanam and leading a gloriously independent life. I've even prayed for death for both of us."

"Gopu, I can't tell you how intensely sorry I am. Though I'm so close, I never even dreamt you were undergoing such torture. You're born to riches, and I thought you and your wife were supremely happy, like Rati and Manmatha. I've never been so wrong in my judgment. Only now do I understand what Thackeray meant when he said that a different world exists under each hat, and that each man is an independent island in the sea of creation."

"Our elders say, with reason, that bedroom secrets should never be divulged. That's why I didn't broach this subject all these days. Had I confided in you, you would have been upset," Gopalan continued, "You're very intelligent, but what's needed is an understanding born of experience. Of what use is wealth? Its possession doesn't mean happiness. I think Rati and Manmatha could not have shared the understanding Harishchandra had with Chandramati, an understanding revealed at that moment when, duty bound in the service of an untouchable, he was prepared to draw his sword against her. As Thiruvalluvar has said, It's not mere physical relationship, but the union of minds and genuine mutual understanding that are important. Auvaiyar has also said that happiness follows only from a union of outlook. If that's not established, either the husband or the wife should totally surrender to the other's will. Ideally, both should have the good sense and understanding to share each other's burdens, and be life partners in the true sense. No one can be more unfortunate than the man married to a wife totally incompatible. The problems that would follow from such a situation can end only with death. The rootless life of a thadi brahmachari is far more preferable. If one cannot follow accepted tenets and do good as he can, of what use is his free will? He's no better than the beggar's performing monkey. As Auvaiyar has said, it is better to take sanyasam than live with an incompatible wife."

"Stop it Gopu. If you talk so bitterly, how are you going to pull on? I believe in patience and persistence. Even an ant's movements can wear out a stone. Don't let your depression get the better of you. Let her have her way, but reason gently and change her slowly."

"All right, I shall do as you suggest. Let's see if there's any change. I don't have any hopes, though."

Then, as it was very late, they hurried home.

I have no experience in business but my partner is well versed in the timber trade.

B lessings to my nephew Chiranjeevi Nanu, may all prosperity be his. By the grace of Sri Subramanya, all are well here. Please write frequently about your wellbeing.

Sowbagyavathi Padmavati came of age yesterday, Thursday, after 7:00 am in Simha lagnam. As your mother-in-law's confinement was due soon, I decided to have the rutu santhi immediately, choosing an auspicious muhurtham within a fortnight. However, quite unexpectedly, your mother-in-law delivered a male child this morning. Both mother and child are well. So the rutu santhi has to be postponed to a later date. I'm thinking of arranging it when you come here for your college holidays. I hope you've received the money order for fifteen rupees sent last week.

It's been a poor harvest. The price of paddy has gone up to ten rupees per kottai, and seems likely to rise further. I drew a chit some ten days ago and thought of clearing my outstanding debt with that money. But the loan carries a low rate of interest and my creditor is not pressurizing. So I thought of stocking some paddy. Around this time, a vessel bearing timber docked at Irangal and a sound businessman sought my partnership. Investing our capital and some loans, we have jointly bought around two thousand rupees worth of stock and set up a timber shop in Irangal only the day before yesterday. There's promise of good profit. I have no experience in business but my partner is well versed in the timber trade.

There's no other news. Please start immediately after your college closes, even if Gopala Iyer doesn't accompany you. Do reply in detail.

Aasirvadams,

By the grace of Lord Subramanya,

Ayyavier, Chirukulam.

Narayanan was overjoyed with the news because it meant his wife's education could be restarted. Gopalan teased him relentlessly.

Narayanan was no longer the boy we first met but a strapping young man of twenty, knowledgeable in the ways of the world. Though well aware of the temptations to which young men like him succumbed, he himself had no bad habits. His passion for music brought some contact with playboys and even prostitutes. But his poverty, combined with his high moral standards, ensured that such dangerous acquaintances did not affect him. Besides, living with Gopalan was a strong deterrent to any dalliance. Gopalan was tone deaf. To him, the melody of a raga and the roar of waves were one and the same. Married to a lovely girl and deeply in love with her, Gopalan was not in the least inclined to seek pleasure elsewhere or accompany Narayanan to music concerts in the homes of prostitutes. It was difficult for Narayanan to set out on his own. His mother, Seethai Ammal, worried constantly that his love for music would cause him to be ensnared by prostitutes, and kept a close watch.

Narayanan, well aware of this, begged permission for some outstanding concerts, and sometimes even resorted to lies, resulting in occasional misunderstanding with Gopalan. When transported by excellent music, that too coming from a beautiful woman, his native good sense was momentarily displaced by a flood of desire. Once, after the veena concert of a prostitute in Pavalakkara Street, he was so overcome with passion that he entirely forgot he had vowed, before the sacred fire, not to touch a woman other than his dharmapatni Padmavati and took leave of all sense of shame. For a whole day he was like one possessed, unable to eat or sleep, and finally was emboldened to enquire about the lady. Learning he could not even approach her house without twenty rupees, he was distraught, and pitied himself for his poverty. He decided to approach Gopalan for a loan ... he, who had once given an exposition in the college Tamil Sangam on the kural about the evil effects of illicit relationships. Lost in the dreams of the pleasures in store for him, a thought flashed across, dispelling all such lowly imaginings ... Savithri's reactions to the news of his misbehaviour. Even the certainty of the distress his action would cause his mother, uncle and wife did not affect him as deeply as the fear that Savithri, who quite contrary to custom had come to accept him as a brother, would spurn him in disgust. The high esteem in which he held Savithri acted as a check on his base thoughts and desires. For no one else did he have the same high, affectionate regard. He considered Savithri his guardian angel and thoughts of her were a sort of talisman protecting him from going astray.

Savithri herself had no inkling of Narayanan's worshipful attitude or the role she played in guarding his virtue. The only comfort she sought in her tragic plight was in the company of her little nephew. She patiently put up with Kalyani's tantrums and harsh words and tried to correct her through example and advice. Her speech was always sweet and soft and her genuine concern for others predominated her personal tragedy.

On the evening of the day the letter from Ayyavier arrived, Narayanan and Gopalan went to the beach. The ocean always fascinated Narayanan, and he imagined that he shared a special relationship with it. The magnificent sight of huge waves rolling onto the shore never failed to fill him with awe. He compared the immense swell of the waves, diminishing while approaching the shore and ending with a quiet spread on the sands, to the bombast of vain fools fading away when confronted by the truly learned. He poetically likened the constant roar of the ocean to the complaints of Bhooma

Devi to the Almighty informing Him of the sorrows and sufferings of her inhabitants. When at the beach, he invariably spent some time in silent contemplation. As he sat thus, Gopalan said, "Dé Nanu! Remember your lecture at my rutu santhi? Now you'll be having yours within two months of your wife's coming of age. What happened to your two-year resolve?"

Narayanan was startled out of his reverie. He said, "I've agreed to this only after deep thought. There are many reasons. First of all is the wish of my mother and others. I think Padmi herself would prefer this and if I don't agree, she might begin to imagine I don't care for her. Women need to live with their men. Don't you remember the verse in *Jeevaka Chintamani* which says that women, endowed with sensuous instincts, find pleasure only with their husbands? Secondly, only after the rutu santhi can I bring her over here and continue her education. This, to me, is in itself a sufficient reason. Thirdly, Amma is not very well and unable to work as before. Even cooking for the two of us is too much of a strain. Fourthly, this is a harsh world. If I don't follow custom, all sorts of things will be said about me. After all, it should be possible to pay attention to health and physical development and not be governed by lust alone."

Gopalan intervened, continuing in the same vein, "Fifthly, I am also growing older, sixthly, she has matured. Seventhly, this is a tropical country and the requirements specified by doctors apply only to cold countries like England. Eighthly, my naughty mind troubles me when I attend music concerts by prostitutes. Poda, don't I know? Your logic and reasoning vary according to circumstances."

"But you'll come, won't you? I did come to your rutu santhi. The college will be closed. What'll you do here?"

"Yes, I'm also thinking of leaving. I want to be separated from Kalayanam for some time. It's getting worse and she is driving me crazy. My plan is to go to Ariyur first, then for all of us to attend your rutu santhi and thereafter to go over to Kutralam. You and your wife must join us there. It's the ideal spot for newly weds. After the holidays, I'll leave Kalyanam at her father's and return to Madras with Savithri Akka."

"How strange! Here I am, lining up arguments for bringing my wife over, while you're making out a stronger case for separation from yours! Personally, I feel I'll be able to study harder if Padmi comes over."

"Don't make me envious. Look at your hand. Are all the fingers alike? To each his fate, that's all there's to it. Let's drop the subject."

They spent a long while in silence, each with his thoughts, before starting for home.

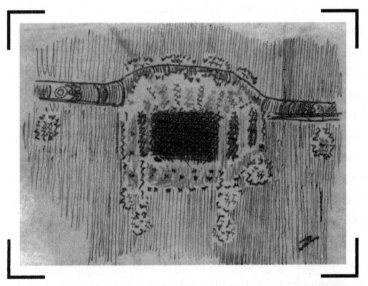

No one in the town had ever seen the likes of the flower bedecked palanquin in which the girl was taken around.

The grand celebration of the coming of age ceremony of Padmavati, daughter of Chirukulam Ayyavier, in particular the procession on the day of the rutu snanam, was praised even by his enemies. No one in the town had ever seen the likes of the flower bedecked palanquin in which the girl was taken around. Its decoration had taken two whole days and nights and garlands had been brought from Tirunelveli. This deprived the neighbourhood temples of flowers even for the main archanai and Mahavishnu and Sivaperuman had to be content with tulasi and vilvam leaves. Flowers were brought from as far away as Tenkasi, six kaadams away. Periya Subbu, the vidwan who had not performed even at the marriage in Periya Pannai Krishna Iyengar's family, was brought over by Ayyavier to play the nadaswaram during his daughter's procession. When a girl comes of age, the common practice is to distribute some pittu. But who ever heard the likes of Ayyavier distributing one padi of London cheeni to each household? The young girls of the area are generally reluctant to stay with a girl who comes of age, because usually, only the dropped cash is shared amongst them. But when Ayyavier made it known he would put in twenty rupees apart from the dropped cash, even the daughters of his enemies and girls from Irangal came over for the stay. And the grandeur of the celebration itself, the music, the joyous clamour, the astounding fireworks, the feast! The melody of the raga Bhairavi, divinely played by Periya Subbu, still lingers in my ears. The expenses would have totalled no less than six hundred rupees.

As his wife went into labour soon after his daughter came of age, Ayyavier had to put off the rituals till the second menstrual cycle. Though his debts were steadily rising, Ayyavier had other considerations in mind. Padmavati was, after all, his only daughter, and there was the argument of his wife, upholding the maxim commonly accepted by Hindus in their daily life, that it is best not to subject expenditures such as these to detailed, item-wise analysis. There was, besides, the desire to revel in his newfound status as a timber merchant. So Ayyavier borrowed heavily and spent lavishly, winning the acclaim of the entire town. And why shouldn't I praise him? After all, I got enough quality sugar to last my household needs for three months, my five daughters received two annas each, while my wife got four annas, and even the baby was given one anna. My wife and children were fed sumptuously for four days while I enjoyed one grand feast, brilliant fireworks and delightful music. I should certainly praise the man who was behind all this. When I consider that all the enjoyment was, quite literally, at his expense and with a sharp increase in his indebtedness, I do feel a stab of pity for the man, though not without some secret relish.

Not that Ayyavier was unconcerned about the increase in his debts. The main reason why he decided to marry his daughter to his nephew was to minimize wedding expenses. At that time, his wife was not very enthusiastic. Her plan to get her nephew Kittu as her son-in-law had failed and her animosity towards her sister-in-law, Seethai Ammal, was still strong. But this had waned over time and she had reached a happy frame of mind, what with her newborn child and pride in her son-in-law studying for his BA in Madras. Furthermore, it is usually the husband who receives praise for the success of a

---

Rutu snanam: The ritualistic bath given after a girl comes of age. **Stay With a girl**: Women are considered impure and are required to be segregated during their periods. It was the practice, when a girl came of age, to get some girls of the area to keep her company during the segregation. **Dropped Cash**: During such stay, the girls amuse themselves by singing and taking part in folk dances like Kummi. Visitors encourage them by dropping some cash which is later shared by the girls.

wedding ceremony. But with other celebrations like rutu snanam and valaikappu, which come under the purview of the lady of the house, it is she who earns the respect of the women of the town. And so it was that Ayyavier's wife got him round to celebrations on so grand a scale.

Some may find it hard to believe that Ayyavier, who once was at loggerheads with his wife and even given to beating her, could have become so amenable to her wishes. But such doubts will disappear when the nature of domestic relations is examined. How long can a couple, living under the same roof and in the constant company of each other, sustain mutual animosity? In course of time, there would come about a sort of working understanding, if not a true union of minds. The weaker partner would be gradually subdued. An aggressive person, perennially on the offensive, is treated with a sort of respect. Those too lazy to maintain continued opposition would easily tire of confrontation, while the timid would always prefer compromise. As a learned man has remarked, the majority in any society are either lazy or timid, and so the aggressive are always able to have their way.

It also seems natural for most men to abide by the wishes of their women. As it is not possible for women to get all things done through their own effort, they are endowed with the wiles and skill for getting men to accomplish them. Even if it comes about that fish have to teach their young to swim, women will not need instructions in the art of getting round men. Not even the Gayatri, the ultimate among mantras, is as strong as a curtain lecture, which few men can withstand. A determined woman can always accomplish whatever she has set her heart on. In this regard, the persistence of women is truly remarkable. As for the man, his one dear wish, after the travails and tensions of earning a livelihood, is for peace and quiet at home. For

Ayyavier, apart from these general conditions, there was also a special reason to gratify his wife's wishes. She had just borne him the son he had long wanted. So he decided to bear the risk of a rising debt burden.

After the celebration of the puberty ceremony, Ayyavier set about the arrangements for the rutu santhi – getting the necessary jewels, vessels, et cetera. He wrote to Narayanan, giving the date of the muhurtham and asking him to start as soon as his college closed.

Narayanan and Gopalan went out again to a different
scenic spot each day, the various falls or the lovely,
dense, wood-shrouded places.

M ere words cannot describe the beauty of Kutralam. If you wish to forget all the cares you have inherited and want to experience pure, unsullied joy, proceed to Kutralam and gaze at the waterfalls, bearing in mind the fact that sight is a marvellous blessing you are endowed with. Should your burden of care not ease, there's just one remedy left. Climb the steps behind the falls that go up the hillock, jump headlong into Pongumankadal and be swept down with the water. If you do not know how to swim, you don't even have to take the trouble of climbing the steps. Just choose a moment when no one is around and jump into the pool at the foot of the falls.

Our friends are all here. Narayanan and Gopalan are sitting under the falls, shrouded by the misty spray, the force of the water acting as a restful massage. If we follow the direction of their glances whenever they emerge for a breath of air, we see Kalyani and Padmavati splashing water on each other in the pool below. On a rock over there sits Seethai Ammal, dressed in naarmadi, the special raw silk considered pure and worn by orthodox widows, with vibhuti smeared on her person and rudraksha malais around her neck. Oblivious to the clamour around her — the roar of the waterfalls, the shouts of the bathers, the sound of musical instruments from the temple, the chatter of monkeys — she sits with eyes closed, hands folded in prayer and lips moving in silent chanting, the embodiment of piety, engrossed in namaskara japam. Savithri too is totally unaware of her surroundings or of the pitiful glances she, a beautiful young woman in naarmadi, attracts from passersby. She is completely absorbed in her little nephew whom she holds in her arms, pointing out to him the antics of the monkeys that jump around, snatching fruits and coconuts from the bathers and fighting with each other for these spoils. The child's joy at this spectacle is transferred to her and she loses herself in it. Is there anything in this world that can equal children in helping us forget, giving us joy?

It has been a long time since we last saw our heroine, Padmavati. She's now grown up, but the glow of innocence and the happiness on her face makes her still seem a little girl. Though it is less than a fortnight since her rutu santhi, she does not wear much jewellery, whether to please her husband or for fear of the force of the water, we cannot say. But no one looking at her would say that jewels would further enhance her looks. Jewellery worth a lakh of rupees cannot equal the pleasure the natural beauty of her face gives the beholder.

Seeing that her mother-in-law had finished her japam, Padmavati came out of the pool, dried her hair and wrung out their wet clothes. Following this, Kalyani also came out, and after a while, Savithri gave the child to her and had her bath. Then they all set forth first for the darshanam of the deities of Kutralam, Kurumbaleeswarar and Kuzhalvaiammai, and then homewards to the rented bungalow, playfully throwing the prasadam of coconut and fruit to the monkeys on the way.

All of them lived in the same bungalow, the expenses being mostly borne by Gopalan. They usually went to the main falls early in the morning and spent a long time there, bathing and enjoying themselves. Then back home and after a meal, Narayanan and Gopalan went out again to a different scenic spot each day, the various falls or the lovely, dense wood-shrouded places like Ilanji and Tenkasi. Some time of the day was also spent in studies and in the evenings they once again wandered around to return tired and fall sound asleep after dinner. Seethai Ammal was always to be found at the falls or at the temple. Narayanan had taught her a verse in praise of the presiding deity and she constantly repeated it to herself.

> *Before Kalan comes,*
> *Before my eyes dim,*
> *Before kith and kin lament over me,*
> *Before I'm burnt on the pyre,*
> *Let me recall your name, Kutralathane!*

Savithri, when not occupied with household chores, played with her little nephew, so much so that people seeing the child always astride her hip, began to wonder if he was grafted on to it. When Kalyani was not with her husband, she spent the time sleeping or playing games. As for Padmavati, her preoccupation, as always, was to anticipate her husband's wishes and please him in every possible way. In this, she was fortunate to have a great natural advantage. Seethai Ammal never interfered in any way with her son and daughter-in-law and allowed them full freedom. Unlike some (most?) mothers-in-law, she was not jealous or possessive. Padmavati did not have to wait for her absence for an opportunity to talk to her husband. If her husband called her, she did not have to hide herself and respond with a mouse-like screech. When something had to be given to her husband, she did not have to place it some distance from him and scuttle back. She could attend to her husband's requirements openly, even in the presence of her mother-in-law. She could, on her own, give her husband the things he liked. She could go to her husband's bedroom without seeking her mother-in-law's permission. She could even help herself to ghee while eating. Need anything more be said? When travelling in a bullock cart, she did not have to sit in front with the cartman, with a screen separating her from her husband. If she wished, she could spend time talking to her husband alone in their room even during the day. Seethai Ammal paid no attention whatsoever to such matters. She was not given to peeping through keyholes or eavesdropping when her son and daughter-in-law were alone. Actually, she would go nowhere near their room. If something had to be done urgently, she would do it herself, rather than summon her daughter-in-law. And all this not out of any sense of resignation or bitterness. It was her genuine wish that her son and daughter-in-law should not suffer as she had but live happily. This was also the essence of her daily prayer. If any woman accused her of being excessively liberal with her daughter-in-law, she would argue that the lawfully wedded wife of her son was entitled to full freedom, and no woman would harass her daughter-in-law if she were only to recall her own sufferings under her mother-in-law. Another of her arguments was that men sought the company of prostitutes only to escape tension arising from the conflict between their wife and mother.

So it was that Padmavati was supremely happy with her husband, their love increasing every day, so much so that she began to wonder if there could be a girl luckier than her in the whole world.

When Seshier's carriage arrived, Gopalan and Narayanan were studying upstairs.

As they were thus happily spending their holidays in Kutralam, salubrious alike to the body and the mind, Gopalan's father Seshier decided to visit his son and enjoy a holy bath as well. He arrived with his family on the day before amavasai. While they were all very happy to see him, his condition had become pitiable. He who had once been feared and respected, striding like a tiger both at home and in the town, now looked like an ensnared gazelle. His children were deeply hurt that he'd become a laughing stock. The marriage broker Ayyasami vathiar was also one of the party. This man had, for two years, been a member of Seshier's household. He and Seshier's mother-in-law, the English widow Kamakshi Ammal, were on intimate terms. He also shared a clandestine relationship with Kamalambal, Seshier's wife. These two women were of dubious chastity, and Seshier's domestic life was in shambles. The vathiar was always to be found in the company of the two women. If they were in the kitchen, he was at its doorstep. If they were at the bathing ghat in the canal, he was a few steps away. If they were in the ladies' line at the temple, he was in the men's line, facing them. Poor Seshier was too innocent and guileless to comprehend all this. The whole town, except Seshier, knew the truth about the vathiar. He himself was quite open about it. When friends teased him he would only say laughingly, "Oh, get on with you! These two good women are taking such good care of me that I don't miss my late wife in the least. Can you find such kindly souls in the world?" Even if any suspicion had arisen in Seshier's mind, he would have never gathered the courage to question his formidable mother-in-law. Compared to her, even the shrewish rakshasis of legends were good and gentle women. He was so totally besotted with his wife that even the sight of her and the vathiar together failed to plant a seed of suspicion in his mind. And thus the vathiar and the two women continued their happy coexistence.

Seethai Ammal had heard about these matters from Narayanan and, not desiring any contact with these *pure* women, decided to leave for Tirumalai the day before they were expected for the darshanam of Sri Subramanya, taking her daughter-in-law with her. No extent of pleading by Gopalan could change her mind and she remained unusually adamant. Finally, she heeded Gopalan's plea that Savithri and Kalyani would on their own have too hard a time, while the presence of an outsider might have a subduing effect on Kamakshi Ammal and agreed to leave Padmavati behind. But she herself went away and did not return to Kutralam even for the holy amavasai bath.

When Seshier's carriage arrived, Gopalan and Narayanan were studying upstairs while Savithri, Padmavati and Kalyani were downstairs playing with Raja. Hearing the bells of the bullock cart, they all came out. Even before entering the house, Kamakshi Ammal said in an imperious tone, "Savithri! Is there any milk for Baby Durai Raja?" (This was the pet name of the second child born to Seshier's wife). Savithri said very softly, "What a pity! I was afraid the leftover milk might spoil and so gave it to the child only a little while ago." Kamakshi Ammal ordered, "There's bound to be some, just look again. This child too is an heir. Don't tell lies. This janma of yours has been ruined. In the next one at least your lot should be better, shouldn't it?" This remark hurt and enraged Gopalan and Narayanan. But what could they say, when Seshier stood by silently, head bowed? Padmavati and Kalyani were disgusted and went into the house with Gopalan's child. Savithri controlled her anger and agony and said quietly, "Why do you say that, Amma? If you think I'm lying, please go to the kitchen and check for yourself. Is not Durai Raja our child too? Besides, would anyone deliberately deny milk to a child? I'll send the maid for some fresh milk right away."

As they entered the house Padmavati eagerly put out her arms to the child Kamalambal was carrying. That lady scowled and turned away saying, "He won't go to you. Just play with your own children, that'll do." She then left the child with the vathiar. The next day, Durai Raja developed a slight cough because of the strain of the journey and the change in the climate. His mother and grandmother immediately started a tirade against those whose evil eye had affected the child. Raining all manner of hideous curses – Some frightful witches have cast their evil eyes! May they go blind! May their entire tribe rot and perish! May they suffer agonies in all their janmas! May they eat their own children – they took a heap of dry chillies and salt, waved it round the child's head three times, and threw it into the open fire. Besides putting out the fire, this caused endless coughing and sneezing all round.

When Gopalan had visited Ariyur for a week, prior to Narayanan's rutu santhi, he had not found an opportunity to talk to his father in private as he was too depressed by the situation in the house. His father too had shown no inclination for any conversation and in fact avoided it. Now, Gopalan wanted to discuss some matters with him and sought him out when he was alone in a room.

He started by asking if there was any news of Sangu and if it was not necessary to pursue the search. Seshier replied, "Why don't you do it yourself? I've done enough searching. Maybe that donkey is dead."

After a short silence, Gopalan continued, "Our vacation will be over soon. This time, I am thinking of leaving her behind at her parents' and taking only Savithri Akka with me. My studies are affected."

"Do so," said Seshier. "But why should your wife go to her parents? She should stay with us. She hasn't spent even a month at our house. Let her stay with us."

Even before he had finished, Kamakshi Ammal, who was outside eavesdropping, entered the room saying, "No need for anyone to come to Ariyur. Let everyone stay in their own place."

Seshier recoiled, trembling like a snake before a kite, and said softly, "All right. Do as you wish." Gopalan could not take up any other matter but secretly blessed Kamakshi Ammal for the help she had rendered.

While talking to Savithri that evening Gopalan said, "I used to think that black magic, casting spells and the like were all rubbish. Now I believe there's some truth in them. Looks like Appa may go completely mad quite soon."

"Ambi! It's no use blaming anyone. It is our fate. Remember the verse from *Kamba Ramayanam* that Nanu quotes so often, the one in which Rama placates an angry Lakshmana as they set out for the forest,

> *It is not the fault of the river when it runs dry,*
> *So too, it is neither the king, nor our lady mother,*
> *Nor the prince who is to blame,*
> *The fault lies with our fate.*

If that is what Sri Rama himself experienced, where do we ordinary mortals stand?"

Now he began to teach her English. Since she had a good
grounding in Tamil, she learnt it with ease.

When our friends returned to Madras after their vacation, Kalyani did not accompany them. Gopalan was unusually firm and managed to leave her and the child at her father's house. Savithri came along with him to cook and keep house. Narayanan came with his wife and mother and as before, occupied a part of the house.

While she was at her parents' house, Padmavati had not allowed herself to forget what she had learnt. Though unable to proceed on her own, she went over all that had been taught and also learnt by heart the poetry Narayanan had marked in her book. Now he began to teach her English. Since she had a good grounding in Tamil, she learnt it with ease. Narayanan believed that unless a wife could fully share her husband's joys and sorrows, she could not be considered a companion for life. His cherished desire was that his wife should appreciate the beauty of English literature and be able to share the immense delight he derived from the plays of Shakespeare, the poetry of Tennyson and the like. He did not in the least want her to master abstruse learning. According to him, a wife should be able to manage the household well and provide the necessities for a healthy life for her husband and children, and also have the learning to broaden her outlook through reading good literature, history and the like. All this, he felt, was entirely feasible and an average woman could rise to this level, provided she had the interest and application. But learning beyond this for an average housewife was, in his view, totally impractical. As for Padmavati, besides wanting to please her husband, as always, she was also very enthusiastic about learning a new language. She picked up her books whenever she had a moment to spare and became quite enamoured of the English language, developing at the back of her mind a slight contempt for the language she knew well and was her own. To her husband, she listed in jest the advantages she would gain through a knowledge of English – he would not be able to berate her and discuss her with Gopalan in a language she could not understand and he could no longer casually brush aside her queries about the letters in English he received from friends. All this delighted Narayanan and increased his enthusiasm for teaching. He felt immensely sorry for Gopalan who was forced to be separated from his difficult wife and lead a lonely life. This thought made him appreciate his own good fortune all the more.

Padmavati's presence did not affect Narayanan's studies. On the other hand, it increased his comfort. Rising early she would clean the house and utensils and in accordance with her mother-in-law's requirements of ritualistic purity, bathe, and then cook a meal before Narayanan left for the college. During this time Narayanan and Gopalan would be studying together. While they were at college, Padmavati and Savithri would read some Tamil book to Seethai Ammal. If Savithri was so engaged, Padmavati would work on her English. Or while Seethai Ammal had a nap, the two of them would play some game. After returning from college, Narayanan would spend half an hour teaching his wife. Then he and Gopalan would go out to play or spend time on the beach. Occasionally, the night meal would be readied early and all of them would go to the beach together. Usually after dinner, from 7:30 or 8:00 to 9:00 or 9:30 pm, Narayanan would be with his wife, sometimes teaching her a new lesson or a song. Then she would go to sleep and he was free to study for as long as he wanted. As usual, he would get up early and study. Sometimes Padmavati would also study her lessons along with him. She attended to all the household chores happily and diligently, maintaining a neat, clean home, dusting the books frequently, keeping everything in its appropriate place, attending to all her husband's needs, washing and folding his clothes, mending them and giving them to the vannan when necessary, and keeping accounts, airing the bed clothes, cleaning all the lanterns and having them ready with oil and wick, helping her husband in his personal needs such as with his oil bath and in combing his hair, getting him his books when necessary after carefully spelling out their English titles, and promptly responding when her mother-in-law or husband called her. Hence Narayanan was free of all minor irritants and was able to give his studies more attention than before. There was, however, one wish he was unable to fulfil. His long felt desire was to teach Padmavati music, vocal as well as some instrument. But that was not possible. It was unthinkable that a man could be her teacher and among women, only prostitutes were equipped to teach music. Apart from the fact that getting one as a teacher for Padmavati was too revolutionary an idea, totally opposed to custom, it would also entail an expense he could not afford. So he consoled himself with the thought that the wish could be fulfilled in the future, once he started earning. He and his wife were deeply in love and supremely happy.

The separation from Gopalan's child affected Savithri very much, and she felt as if she had lost her mangalyam all over again. However, moving with Seethai Ammal everyday, she began to develop an interest in spiritual matters, and her thoughts turned to acts of charity and service.

For some unexplainable reason, I am scared. I fear some disaster will follow.

While our friends were thus leading a life engrossed in studies they heard about a drama troupe performing in the city. They did not pay much attention to this at first, so strong was the imprint of their unforgettable experience, like the proverbial cat that had tasted hot milk. But temptation reared its head when they heard the praises and ecstatic accounts of their classmates who had seen the shows and proclaimed them excellent. A visit to the venue confirmed it was fireproof, safe and big enough to accommodate the huge crowds that thronged there every day. When he heard that the troupe included a nine year old boy who sang divinely, the desire to hear him took root in Narayanan's mind. Gopalan's interest was roused by the report that the actor playing female roles surpassed the divine maidens Rambha, Urvasi, Tilottama and Menaka in beauty, and was so convincing in the tragic scenes as to melt even the hardest of hearts.

Much as both of them wished to take their womenfolk to a show, they knew this was impossible. How could Seethai Ammal, who considered it a cardinal sin even to set eyes on a man dressed as a woman and Savithri, who had lost her husband in a drama fire, be persuaded to attend a show? To take only Padmavati was also very difficult, and in any case Seethai Ammal would never permit it. Even the two of them would not be given permission. Assuming Seethai Ammal and Padmavati were to somehow agree, Savithri would not allow it under any circumstance, and neither could openly defy her. Considering all this, they decided to sleep on the thinnai and slip away after everyone was asleep.

Because of his deep love for her, Narayanan revealed their plans to Padmavati. Her reaction was totally unexpected. She was extremely distressed and begged hard, trying her best to prevent his going.

Finally she said, "I'm not afraid of a fire accident, or that a craze for the theatre will affect your studies. For some unexplainable reason, I am scared. I fear some disaster will follow. You told me, didn't you, that in Sindhupoonthurai, the day your father died, you and Amma experienced a strange shivering? Was there any rational explanation for that? I somehow feel this wish of yours is going to lead to something terrible."

Narayanan hugged and kissed her. "Adi kutti Padmi, don't worry. Do you think I might fall in love with some female there? But all the actors are men. Besides, even if Rambha herself appears, would I even glance at her, forgetting my ammanga? You're needlessly nervous. When I get back, I'll knock softly on the door three times, and you'll know that your athaan has returned safe and sound."

"If nothing else," Padmavati persisted, "Is this not duplicity, a lie of sorts, deceiving Amma and Savithri Akka? Remember the story of Othello and how a small deceit by Othello feigning a headache caused a great tragedy, because the handkerchief his wife brought out to soothe him slipped down and finally reached the villain Iago. Haven't you yourself told me how that small lie had led to disaster? How can we ignore the moral of this tale?"

Narayanan couldn't counter this argument but was delighted. Laughing, he kissed Padmavati. "This is why our elders were against educating women!" he quipped. Telling her once again not to worry, he left. And she, who held her husband in reverence, could argue no further, but only utter a silent prayer.

On the pretext that it was sultry, Narayanan and Gopalan went to sleep on the thinnai. Around midnight, when everyone was asleep, they rose, quietly arranged their pillows to suggest a sleeping form and walked briskly to the drama theatre.

The show that night was *Keechaka Vadham*. They purchased the tickets and found seats. Even as they entered they heard a boy singing divinely from behind the scene and Narayanan was completely captivated. The theme of the song was Draupadi's denunciation of Keechaka.

The stage had a beautiful garden as the backdrop. A radiant and lovely Draupadi, like a deer stalked by a predator, was trying to evade a rabid Keechaka, played by a short, stocky man standing like an impassioned tiger. When the song ended, Draupadi spoke, "Adé paavi, chandala, panchamapathaka! How dare you do this? May your head burst! You're the son of a king and yet know nothing of neeti sastra! You karma chandala, neecha!" To which Keechaka replied, "Sabhash, You queen among women! But mere abuse from your tremulous red lips will not do! You should strike me with your soft divine hands. Only then can I realize my life's purpose."

As soon as they heard that voice, Narayanan and Gopalan looked at each other in astonishment. After listening closely for a few minutes Narayanan said softly, "Doesn't it sound like Sangu?" Gopalan was overcome by emotion and his eyes brimmed. They got up silently even before he finished speaking and came out. Narayanan went to the ticket office and asked the man in charge about the actor playing Keechaka. The latter said, "Today the role has been taken by Avittu-puli, Daal-jodi, Sabhash Sankara Iyer." Asked to explain, the man said that the actor was an expert, a puli in the card game of avittu, that the silver studs he wore in his ears were like a pair of brilliant lanterns used in carts, and that he was given to using the expression

---

Keechaka Vadham: Bhimasena's killing of prince Keechaka who tried to molest Draupadi during the Pandava's last year of exile, when they were staying in anonymity in the service of King Virata.

Sabhash very often in his conversation and hence had been endowed with this sobriquet.

Until the play ended, they stood outside discussing further course of action. Enquiries after the crowd dispersed revealed Sangu had been injured in the simulated fight with Bhimasena and was resting inside, unable to move because of a sprained ankle. They went backstage and were shocked by his dishevelled state. Placing him in a carriage, they brought him home.

Looking at Sangu secretly, she trembled as if she beheld a murderous bandit.

S angu could not at first recognize Gopalan, scarred as he was by burns. However, it cannot be said that he was overly upset when he heard how this had come about. But his eyes filled with tears when he learnt of Savithri's tragedy. Reaching home, when he saw her in her widowed state, even his hard heart melted. He hugged her and sobbed in uncontrollable grief. However, this grief was transient and in a very short time his native nature resurfaced.

The next morning all of them surrounded Sangu asking him to tell them about all that had happened after he ran away from home. And this he proceeded to do, shamelessly, without hesitation or restraint. "I was very angry and upset when Appa, in his old age, went away with Ayyasami vathiar for his third marriage, without showing any concern for me or my marriage. I thought of suicide or of another attempt at conversion. At this point, Rama Iyengar, Appa's principal enemy, called me privately and expressed his sympathy. He advised me to demand my share of the property and said that I'd get not less than thirty thousand, with which I could live in luxury. It was then that I realized that ideas of suicide and conversion were pointless. But while I benefited from Iyengar's advice, I didn't want his help in proceeding with my case, for that would give him a hold over me. I decided to look for a vakil on my own and slipped away to Srivaikuntam, taking all my jewellery and the anklet and cash from Akka's trunk. There I sought a vakil and paid twenty rupees for his opinion. I withheld all details and only asked him about my chances of success. He consulted a number of books and finally said that while mine was a difficult case since I was a minor, winning it was not beyond his ability and that he had won a similar case only the previous year. For a fee of two thousand, he said he would argue my case and win it, going up to the High Court on appeal. I told him I didn't have that much money, but he said it did not matter and that I could give him a postdated promissory note for three thousand. This, he said, he would accept as the equivalent of two thousand on hand. I was given a feast at his house that day. Since I'd sneaked out secretly in the clothes I was wearing, I needed a change of dress and so wanted to shop for silk veshtis, shirts, et cetera. The money I had in hand was not enough and so I decided to sell a jewel. I found a goldsmith's shop and brought out only Akka's golusu, hiding the other jewels. The goldsmith asked me various questions while he weighed and examined the golusu. But I was very careful with my replies and did not give away anything. He went into the house saying he needed a touchstone, and returned giving loud instructions to an assistant to go and find out the prevailing price of the sovereign. That fellow returned with two policemen and I was scared stiff. They closed the door and searched my person, finding all the jewels. They threatened me saying the jewels were connected with a theft case in Srivalliputhur, and that I was likely to get a seven year prison term. They paid no attention to my protests and began to beat me, one of them holding a knife at my throat, lest I cried out. Meanwhile, the Head Constable arrived via the goldsmith's backyard. They all got together and told me if I wished to escape with my life, I should leave that very night for Tiruvananthapuram, giving them all the jewellery and keeping only the cash on hand, with one of their men acting as my escort, to ensure I made no report. I agreed to all their instructions thankful that my life was spared. My escort was a Maravan who looked like Yama's messenger. He had a gun and a sickle hidden in his veshti, and told me he would shoot me the minute I caused the slightest suspicion. He didn't leave my side even for a moment. The only food I had was what he got me, beaten rice, peanuts, bananas, coconut milk, curd, et cetera. When we reached Tiruvananthapuram, he left me, warning that he would keep a watch on my activities and wouldn't hesitate to kill me in case of any suspicion. The very next day, I found myself an acchikutti, a young Keralite girl, gave her a mundu and lived happily with her, eating in the ootuporai. Considering what the lawyer had told me and the events that followed, as well as the comforts of Kerala life, I decided to enjoy myself in Kerala for three or four years, until I became a major and then file a case for the property. To avoid recognition, I kept away from people, cut my hair, used a gopi mark on my forehead and changed my name to Padmanabhan. The balance ten rupees I had, I changed to a gold coin and kept safely for future emergencies. While thus living pleasurably with Kunju Baghavathi, one day I heard a voice from the nextdoor acchi's house which sounded like Athimber's. Finding out that it was indeed Athimber I decided to leave Tiruvananthapuram immediately. But the ten rupees I had was not enough for the journeys I had in mind, to places like Bombay. So, to recompense myself for the free pleasure I'd given Kunju Baghavathi, I took eighty seven rupees from her uncle's trunk and left that very night."

Gopalan, listening silently this far despite intense pain and disgust, said, "Enough. Don't go into details of your grand exploits. Should a policeman overhear, there'll be trouble. Cut your story short."

"Why, Anna! You must be hungry. But there isn't any point in going into details. You are unlikely to appreciate what I can tell you about Bombay, Goa, Poona, Hyderabad and Calcutta, of the wonders, the entertainment and the beautiful women of these places, particularly the glorious prostitutes of Goa. All this would be an utter waste, like blowing a conch into a deaf man's ear. Anyway, after my delightful wanderings I reached Madras only three months ago. I happened to meet the members of a drama company whom I'd known in Tiruvananthapuram. I joined them and my jolly life has continued, with song, dance, card games and prostitutes. In four or five months, I'll attain majority and then go home and start proceedings. I'll get my share of the property if my name is Avittu-puli Daal-jodi Sabhash Sankara Iyer. My idea is to start a drama company of my own and make it more famous than Bombay's Indra Sabha. It was providence that I met you. I'm no longer crazy about marriage. Only a fool would stick to one woman and put up with a household of screaming kids when one can have Wives all over. I certainly know how to live, once I have the money!"

This exposition disgusted and disturbed our friends. As for Padmavati, the emotion that predominated was fear. Looking at Sangu secretly, she trembled as if she beheld a murderous bandit. Seethai Ammal left, closing her ears and murmuring "Sivasiva." Gopalan and Narayanan were angry and depressed. Savithri sat head bowed, chin in hand and eyes streaming. As silence reigned, Sangu took out a silver snuffbox, inhaled a pinch and began singing a ditty, not in the best of taste, in praise of money.

After a while, they tried to reason with him, in different ways — begging, praising, pleading, scorning and scolding — advising him to abandon his way of life, get married and give up the idea of engaging their father in a legal battle over the property. Gopalan finally realized that these efforts were all in vain. Considering his father's pitiable state and the chaotic condition of his household, he asked Sangu to give up the idea of a court case and said that he would himself arrange for a peaceable partition of the property. Sangu agreed and Gopalan wrote a detailed letter to their father the same day.

Hearing the movement, Padmavati looked up in alarm and Sangu urgently signalled to her to come out.

Perversity and lechery were predominant in Sangu's speech and deportment. The evil streak in his character had grown stronger because of his close association with gamblers, musicians, entertainers, playboys and prostitutes. His conversation was always impudent and supercilious and he stared openly at every passing woman. He frequently repeated a saying to the effect that ten was the limit of chastity, elaborating that a woman was chaste only up to the age of ten and that there was no woman who could not be bought for ten rupees. This sort of coarse and lewd talk, even in the presence of elders like Seethai Ammal and his older sister and brother caused them revulsion and anger. But they put up with it, fearing that any sign of displeasure might prompt him to go away again and start a legal battle with his father.

Within two or three days of his arrival, his salacious nature began to show, not merely in his conversation but in his actions as well. Lying down in the hall, unable to walk because of his ankle injury, he called out to Padmavati as she passed by, asking her to get him some water, knowing full well that tradition forbade her to speak to him. She hurried to Savithri and said, "Your brother seems to want you." Savithri came to enquire and brought him water. After this incident, Padmavati avoided going anywhere near him, keeping to the edge of the room and hurrying through when this was not possible. But Sangu persisted in his evil intent and lay in wait for an opportunity, like a cat watching a mouse. He leered obscenely when Padmavati happened to glance in his direction, sang vulgar songs and talked at length of his amorous adventures in her hearing. Narayanan noticed all this and was very angry, but said nothing out of consideration for Gopalan and Savithri.

One afternoon, while Narayanan and Gopalan were in college, Seethai Ammal and Savithri were asleep and Padmavati sat by their side studying her English lessons. Sangu got up and slowly made his way to the door of the room. Hearing the movement, Padmavati looked up in alarm and Sangu urgently signalled to her to come out. Thoroughly shaken Padmavati closed her eyes tight and buried her face in her hands too scared even to utter a sound. Sangu then aimed a cowrie shell at her, the touch of which Padmavati mistook for the rascal's hand. This made her cry out, "Amma, Amma!" Seethai Ammal and Savithri woke up with a start and to their enquiries, Padmavati slowly sobbed out the story of Sangu's behaviour, adding that she had felt something touching her back and had surmised it was Sangu, but that it could have been the cowrie shell lying nearby. Meanwhile, Sangu had vanished from the spot and Seethai Ammal and Savithri were too nervous to question him. In the evening, the incident was narrated to Narayanan and Gopalan. When all of them asked Sangu for an explanation, he said he had wanted a drink of water and had called out to Savithri a couple of times. As she'd not come, he had gone up to their room but had not entered it because Padmavati was there. He denied having made any sign to Padmavati but accepted he had thrown the shell, though it was aimed only at Savithri in order to wake her up. He said he had not noticed where the shell had fallen and added, in his usual repugnant manner, that he could not possibly be attracted to Padmavati who could hardly stand comparison with the many beauties who longed for his attention: Kunju Baghavathi of Tiruvananthapuram, Lakshmi Bai of Bombay, Saraswathi Bai of Poona, Chokribi of Hyderabad, Kalyani Devi of Calcutta and Metti Meenal and Veenai Thenal of Patnam.

An enraged Narayanan controlled himself with difficulty and called Gopalan aside to tell him he could not remain a moment longer under the same roof as Sangu. If Sangu could not be asked to get out, he would move out immediately.

Gopalan said, "Nanu, I agree with all that you say and understand your position. I'm now beginning to feel it would've been far better had Sangu perished or remained untraced. He's a menace to our family. But right now, if I chuck him out, he would surely start legal proceedings for the property and our family reputation, already badly damaged, would be completely destroyed. The proposition that I have made to my father is a serious one, and I haven't yet got a firm response. I think I'll get a reply in about ten days. Whatever the decision, Sangu is sure to leave me."

"What you say is right," replied Narayanan. "But a decision is unlikely in ten days. After all, the letter telling you that the matter would be considered has come only today. It'll take at least a month, and I cannot spend even one more day with Sangu. It would also be wrong for Sangu to leave you now. I'll move to another house on this street. We can continue to study together. Don't worry, our friendship will never be affected, and I'll return to live with you the minute Sangu leaves. Please don't worry." Gopalan agreed with reluctance and the very next morning Narayanan and family moved to another house.

Narayanan went to Gopalan's house a few times and always finding him out stopped looking for him and began to take Padmavati to the beach.

For Gopalan, separation from his wife was the cause of both relief and depression. Initially, her absence was as much a hindrance to his studies as her presence had once been. But, in course of time, the pangs of separation abated and he was able to study well. However, this did not last. His mind grew restless and he was emboldened to steal surreptitious glances at the women he met. And if they happened to be young and good looking, he was troubled by lustful thoughts. He was torn asunder by the conflict between good sense and desire. His mind was like a wayward horse. The reins he checked it with were the thoughts of his wife, his love for her and his self-respect. He was ashamed to discuss this problem with his dear friend.

It was in this state of mind that he went to the theatre with Narayanan. The character of Draupadi made a deep impression on him, although he did not quite realize it then because of the shock of the sudden encounter with Sangu. But the impression remained and he was keen to meet the actor who had played the part. On the evening Narayanan moved out, Sangu took Gopalan to that actor. Who had not heard of Sthri-part Seshiengar? Seshiengar was about twenty five, slim, tall, fair, with a graceful gait and rich attire. He had charming features, with expressive eyes that captured attention instantaneously. The appellation, Purusha Mohini, suited him to perfection. Seldom seen without the appurtenances of pleasure, scent and sandal, flowers and betel, and a woman of easy virtue, his face was always lit with a smile unless acting in a scene requiring a tragic mien. He often received expensive presents like gold watches, pearl chains, rings and silks, from rich men who were his fans. There were also women who lost their hearts and gave themselves to him.

The instant he met this exemplary character, Gopalan became his slave. From the very next day, he abandoned games or study in the evenings and, under one pretext or the other, without Narayanan's knowledge, sought the company of Kushal Seshiengar. In a matter of two or three days, the bond of this new friendship seemed two or three janmas strong.

One evening, Seshiengar took Gopalan to the house of his mistress. Unused to such surroundings, Gopalan was hesitant and nervous. But such was the influence of Seshiengar's charm, that he was able to placate his troubled conscience easily. When he entered the house, a great surprise awaited him, for his mistress was none other than Shala, wife of Canal Superintendent Nagamier. Though a widow, she had not shorn her hair and looked very smart, dressed in an expensive Kanchipuram sari and a blouse of Benares silk. She was unable at first to recognize Gopalan, disfigured by burns. When he told her who he was, she immediately recollected the incident in the front hall of Gopalan's Ariyur house and laughingly teased him, singing, "Be off with you, you haughty man, you and I are far apart." Gopalan was delighted with her company. He came to know she was crazy about Iyengar, but that he was unwilling to support her and so would introduce some of his rich friends to her. By then it was getting late, and Gopalan left, promising to return the next day.

While returning home, Gopalan was filled with remorse. He felt he had lost everything at one go – the principles he had followed thus far, the promise he had made to his dear wife not to touch another woman, his speech the previous week at the college Youth Forum on cleanliness of mind and body which had won him wide praise – all these had been allowed to fly away like floss in the wind. He was terribly ashamed of himself and felt it would be better to end his life.

How could he face his wife? He remembered the advice in the New Testament about casting away an offending organ to save oneself. He thought of some options, to tell Narayanan and Savithri and then kill himself, or to confess to Dr Miller who treated him like a son and seek his advice. He spoke to no one at home, hardly ate, locked himself in his room and sobbed until sleep overtook him.

When he woke up the next morning, the happenings of the evening before seemed a dream, the details coming back slowly. The idea of confiding in others or resorting to suicide seemed silly. He decided never to allow himself to stray again. In accordance with that resolve, he did not go seeking Seshiengar that evening, but set out towards the beach by himself. However, Seshiengar came looking for him, saying he had been sent by Shala, who was very keen to see him. Gopalan's good intentions vanished, and he went with Iyengar. He did the same every evening thereafter, telling Savithri he was going out for some games or to the beach.

Gopalan and Narayanan did not meet often outside the college. Gopalan was slightly offended that Narayanan had left his house because of Sangu. Besides that, he was aware of the vast chasm separating Narayanan's friendship and his present relationship. He was aware that what he was doing was wrong, and was unable to interact with Narayanan on the old familiar terms. He felt ashamed and guilty whenever he met him. Narayanan, preoccupied with studies, went to Gopalan's house a few times in the evenings and, always finding him out stopped looking for him, and instead began to take Padmavati to the beach. To keep up appearances, Gopalan went to Narayanan's house when he was sure Narayanan was not at home, and asked Seethai Ammal to tell him about his visit. Thus, for no reason, our two friends began to drift apart.

The letter was addressed to Padmavati Ammal at No ...
Ekambareswarar Street, Patnam.

Sangu was very resentful of Padmavati's rejection of his overtures and her exposure of his behaviour, putting him to shame and earning the anger and disgust of his elders. By nature, he loved causing trouble. Now, he was looking out for appropriate opportunities, intent on harming Narayanan and his family as much as possible.

Sangu was very pleased that a slight breach in his brother's friendship with Narayanan had come about because of him. He now looked for ways of breaking it fully and finally, causing enmity between the two, and to this end, he began bearing all sorts of tales against Narayanan to his brother. Though the break of their friendship would be of no direct benefit to him, he knew very well it would increase Narayanan's financial burden. He noted that the situation was shaping to his advantage and began to scheme ways for greater damage.

Gopalan was under the impression that his brother was not aware of his visits to Shala's house. But Sangu knew everything. He was very close to Iyengar, who assiduously promoted their friendship with the idea of gain when Sangu got his share of the property. Every night, he faithfully reported the day's events to Sangu. Apart from this, Sangu too visited Shala's house.

Gopalan's infatuation with Shala grew day by day. He was completely captivated by her smiling face and charming ways, clever conversation, personal attention like the preparation of special snacks for him, her immediate response to his changing moods, and the amorous play by which she lifted him from depression in a trice. He compared all these with the tensions of his wife's tantrums and tears, which had frequently driven him to the point of contemplating suicide. Within ten days of the relationship, he had presented Shala with clothes and trinkets worth about fifty rupees. But he was not happy about her living like some common prostitute, and wanted to maintain her as his mistress, enjoying her privileges exclusively. To discuss this idea with her, he went to her house twice without Iyengar's knowledge. But both times Shala remained inside and made the servant tell him she was out. Iyengar's orders were that she should see no one without his permission. And while Iyengar's lawfully wedded wife might disobey his orders, never would Shala do so, such was her craze for the man. Frustrated in his attempt, Gopalan wrote Shala a letter, but to no effect.

Returning home from college one evening, Narayanan met the postman who showed him a letter and asked if he knew who it was for. The letter was addressed to Padmavati Ammal at No ... Ekambareswarar Street, Patnam. The number indicated tallied with that of his house and he took the letter, telling the postman that it was for his wife. It surprised him very much. No one but he himself had ever written to Padmavati so far. The stamp showed it had been posted locally. The writing on the envelope resembled Gopalan's handwriting. It was Narayanan's principle that one should not read letters addressed to others, and he would chastise Padmavati even if she read, without his permission, letters from her father addressed to him. Even so, he wanted to have a look at this letter. So he kept it carefully in his pocket and after putting away his books, went to the beach, chose a secluded spot and opened the letter. There was no doubt that the writing inside was Gopalan's, he could have sworn about that. The letter ran thus,

234

Chennai, Ekambareswarar Street, Saturday

My dearest,

As you know very well, I'm your slave. My eyes long for a glimpse of you. I've now come to realize that the affection I had for my wife was false and it's only my love for you that is true. I want to discuss some matters with you in private, so that our love and intimacy can last forever. I came to your house twice, choosing a time when he was not around. But I couldn't meet you and my eyes were denied the blessing of the sight of you. I'll never doubt your feelings for me, I who've heard your loving words and experienced bliss with you. If I were to doubt that, I'd surely perish. I do want to talk to you about plans for our lasting pleasure. Send me a reply immediately, indicating a time when he as well as others won't be at home. You know my address. Should he come while I'm there, I'll manage by saying that I'd actually come to meet him and was waiting for him. Do write immediately. I send you a thousand kisses with this — not one of them an ordinary kiss but each a priceless kiss of ambrosia. The kisses you send in return should be the same.

Ever your dear lover,

Gopu

A part of the paper below the signature was torn off.

Narayanan grew faint as he read the letter and it dropped from his hand. He fell back on the sand in nervous exhaustion. After a while, he got up with a start, picked up the letter and read it over and over again, until each word was indelibly imprinted in his mind. He had absolutely no doubt that it was Gopalan's writing. Only the address was in a slightly different hand, but he decided it was a deliberate blind to prevent suspicion in case someone chanced to see the letter. He recalled his mother telling him about Gopalan's visit twice when he was not at home, which tallied with what was said in the letter. Some expressions used in the letter were also clearly Gopalan's. Certain incidents at Kutralam and in Madras, when he had shared Gopalan's household came to his mind. At that time, his wife's words and Gopalan's behaviour had not roused any suspicion. But they assumed new meaning now. He thought there could be no greater fool than he for failing to see what was actually crystal clear.

This conviction resulted in a wave of uncontrollable anger against the friend who had betrayed him and his faithless wife, and he decided to kill both of them and then commit suicide. He was overcome by sorrow at the thought that he, who had emphasized the vital importance of women's education and domestic harmony, and who had derived great satisfaction in the liberty he had allowed his wife and the joy in her love for him, should have come to this. These thoughts made him sob. He felt sure it was not the burn-scarred Gopalan's looks that had attracted his wife, but his rich attire and affluence. In common with the majority of her sex, she was enamoured of such superficialities. He bitterly regretted his indigence which, more than friendship, had led to his sharing a house with Gopalan. Further, he thought it was not right to suspect the sincerity of Gopalan's friendship as, by nature, he was not a bad man.

His conclusion was that he could not blame Gopalan and that it was only his wife who was responsible for the destruction of their friendship and his life. He recalled some verses by Thayumanavar describing the essential infidelity of women and the dangers of placing any trust in them. "Fear not the poisonous snake or the cyclone or the elephant in musth or hunters or bandits or the messengers of death. But place no trust in the sari clad woman lest you be abandoned." And the poet Pattinathar, "She who stole away to meet her lover while her man slept and crept back quietly to sleep again, how can I trust her, Kacchi Ekambarane?"

He who had once scoffed at such ideas, secure in the belief of his superior intelligence, now felt that only the wisdom of the sages who advocated detachment and renunciation was meaningful.

He spent a long while thus analyzing various alternatives, but could not reach any conclusion. Finally he decided to let things rest and watch further developments, while acting as if he knew nothing. It was past eight o'clock when he finally made his way home.

Seethai Ammal meanwhile was extremely worried that her son, who invariably returned by seven, had not appeared even after the eight o'clock cannon shot. She stood at her doorstep, lantern in hand, anxiously looking up and down the street. She believed Padmavati to be asleep, but she was actually wide awake, convinced that some harm had befallen her husband, and was crying her heart out in the kitchen.

As soon as Narayanan entered, his mother asked him, "You have never been so late. What happened? Did you go somewhere?"

"Yes. I went to a meeting in Mylapore," he lied. As he went to the backyard, Padmavati followed him and in the joy of relief from anxiety hugged him from behind. Without saying a word he pushed her back roughly. Going in again, he told his mother that he had a severe headache and refused food. He allowed her to smear some medicinal paste on his forehead and removing his bed from his bedroom, spread it out in the front passage. Seethai Ammal and Padmavati retired thereafter. Padmavati ate very little and spent a sleepless night, shedding silent tears.

Tears streamed down Padmavati's face as she spoke.

From that day, Narayanan stopped talking to his wife. He stopped teaching her and ignored her whether she wept or went without food. When she tried to help him in the usual course, he snapped at her and brushed her aside. He slept alone in the front passage of the house. He talked very little even with his mother. She clearly saw on his face the reflection of his mental turmoil, and questioned him many times and in many ways. But there never was any proper answer. Narayanan started spending his free time alone at the beach or in his study, where no one dared disturb him. The study was cleaned by Padmavati only in his absence. The occasional visits to Gopalan's house were completely abandoned. He avoided Gopalan and turned aside if he chanced to run into him at college. Gopalan, infatuated with Shala and steeped in the new friendship with Iyengar, found this convenient and behaved accordingly, which served to remove any lingering doubts from Narayanan's mind.

While things stood thus, another letter addressed to Padmavati was delivered by the postman to Narayanan. It ran as follows,

Patnam, Ekambareswarar Street, House No ..., Thursday.

Padmi, my dear love,

I don't know why you haven't replied, although I'm sure I've done no wrong. I never thought, even in my dreams, that you, my dearest, would treat me thus. How can you do this, after our wonderful times together? Perhaps you've forgotten my address or maybe you're not able to get hold of a postal envelope. So I'm enclosing an addressed envelope. Now I hope you'll reply the minute this reaches you. Our exams will be over on Saturday. The family property is to be partitioned and so we're all leaving for our place on Monday. When are you going? I must meet you before we leave. So, do reply immediately. The rest in person. A thousand kisses are sent with this. You've to return these along with those sent earlier – plus interest!

Looking forward to your reply,

Your Gopu

An envelope with Gopalan's address was enclosed. This entire letter was written in a hand similar to the one on the envelope of the previous letter – that is, like Gopalan's writing in deliberate disguise. Narayanan's emotions on reading this letter hardly need description. Once again, he spent a lot of time thinking over the problem, and finally concluded that, since his wife was the wrongdoer, he could take no action against Gopalan, apart from breaking off their friendship. He decided to stay on in Madras for the holidays and to write to his father-in-law, asking him to come over and take Padmavati home, and then to cut off their relationship completely. He felt that to say or do anything more at this point would be foolish, and result in giving unnecessary publicity to his shame. He decided to explain everything to his mother after his wife's departure. The very next day he wrote to his father-in-law, saying that he intended to stay back and study during the holidays, but that as his wife was rather weak and also wanted very much to visit her parental home, he should come immediately and escort her.

On Sunday evening, Gopalan and Savithri came to Narayanan's house to ask if they too intended to travel, and if not, to take leave of them. It so happened that Narayanan was not at home when they came. They waited for a while, but as he did not return and as there was no mention of any travel plans, they left telling Seethai Ammal they would be taking that evening's train.

Narayanan returned very late. Seethai Ammal saw that he looked even more depressed and tired than usual. Sensing that this mood had been caused by some misunderstanding with his wife, she surmised that it would be resolved if they were left alone, and went out saying she wanted to visit the temple. Narayanan went into his room without speaking a word. Padmavati waited for a while in misery and then gathered courage to go to his room. As he continued to ignore her, she thought about a possible conversational opening that would not cause anger but arouse some interest and finally said, "Where were you all this time? Did you go to the station with Gopalanna? He and Savithriakka came here to take leave and waited a long time for you. Then they left as it was getting late for their train. Did you meet Gopalanna at all? He was so keen on meeting you and waited ever so long."

Narayanan snapped, "Was it to see me or you that he came? Why does he have to meet me? You and he would've so much to share and collect interest on kisses."

Though Narayanan spoke with the force of righteous anger, his voice choked and tears welled in his eyes, in spite of himself, as he uttered the last sentence.

Padmavati, utterly shocked, trembled on hearing this. "Aa, what are you saying? I don't understand!"

"Oh, but naturally! How can you understand? Is this not the usual pretence of all women? Do you have to teach a fish to swim? You know nothing of course." Narayanan was bitterly sarcastic.

Tears streamed down Padmavati's face. "What you say scares me. I don't understand anything. You've been so strange lately. I don't know why. I only know I've done no wrong consciously, either in thought or word. You're my god and my only desire is to please you. If I've done any wrong, it's only out of foolishness, and you must correct me, that's your duty. We've been so happy together ... and now? I am devastated by the change. If it's true that you did love me once, just tell me what is my fault."

"Adi neeli, you deceitful wretch, examine your conscience ..." said Narayanan as he took out the first letter from his trunk and gave it to Padmavati. She read the first few lines and said, "This looks like Gopalanna's writing. Why do you want me to read what he has written to some wretched whore?"

"Only to this wretched whore! Look at the envelope! And if you want further proof, look at this, the wretched whore is addressed by name. And you call him Anna!" Narayanan gave her the second letter.

Even as she looked at it, Padmavati swooned. Narayanan splashed some water on her face and she got up, and crying bitterly said she knew nothing, and called on the gods to help her in her innocence. She said she was ready to swear her innocence whichever way Narayanan wanted. Narayanan remained silent at first but finally said, "Stop this pretence! Even if you were to increase it a thousandfold, I won't be impressed. I've been duped, led up the garden path. That's my fate. I've written to your father and he'll be here in about four days. I'll be sending you back with him and with that our relationship in this life will end. So stop all this acting," and left the room.

A little later, Seethai Ammal returned.

It was then that the realization came to him that he was now an orphan, without any support, and he sobbed bitterly for a while.

The day following the events recorded in the last chapter, Narayanan received the following letter.

No 57, Church Street, Karaikal. Sunday.

Blessings to my nephew Chiranjeevi Nanu. All is well. I desire to know your wellbeing. You may be surprised to hear from me from this place. Last Sunday, our timber shop at Irangal was destroyed by fire, causing a loss of over three thousand rupees, including my investment and borrowings. At that time I'd gone to Tirunelveli on some work. Some people say that I've been cheated by my partner, Muthiah Pillai. They report that while I was away, he sold all the timber to his friends for cash or on credit and set fire to the shop himself. But as far as I know, he's not that sort of a person. When I told him about this rumour, he insisted he was innocent, swearing on Ilai Vibhuti. If he's really guilty, he'll be punished by god. You're aware of my earlier borrowings, secured by some of my assets. I'd mortgaged the rest of my property and also borrowed against a promissory note to finance the timber trade. The value of the mortgaged property is not sufficient even to pay the loans against it. My creditors started proceedings against me the day following the fire. I could not bear the thought of declaring insolvency and presenting myself a pauper in the town we've lived in respectability for generations. I was also afraid I might be sent to jail for indebtedness. So I left your mother-

---

Ilai vibhuti: Literally, vibhuti on a leaf. In the Subramanya temple in Tiruchendur, vibhuti prasadam is given in the leaf of a plant grown locally. This is considered so sacred that swearing by it is equivalent to swearing by the Lord of the temple.

in-law at her parents' house and came here stealthily in the
dead of the night. Until I discharge all my debts, by working
as a coolie if need be, I cannot return home. Right now I'm
working as an accountant to a merchant. You must not be
unduly affected by this. I've consoled myself. How can we
fight fate? I'll write in detail about further developments.
Do write often about the wellbeing of all of you. Unless it is
very inconvenient, I think it would be best for you to move
in once again with Gopala Iyer. Give all this news to Akka.
Many aasirvadams. Lord Subramanya's grace,

Yours, Ayyavier (Chirukulam)

A steady stream of tears coursed down Narayanan's eyes as he
read the letter. From the time he had gained awareness, Ayyavier was
the only father he'd known. He had actually been more than a father
to him, lavishing affection and care, giving him and his mother a
home in their dire need, educating him and finally giving him his
dear daughter in marriage. Even now he was helping him with
remittances. Narayanan was filled with remorse when the thought
crossed his mind that the expenses incurred for his education and
other needs was one of the reasons for Ayyavier's present plight. It
was then that the realization came to him that he was now an orphan,
without any support, and he sobbed bitterly for a while. When he
gave his mother the news, she broke down. That good woman's love
for her younger brother was very deep. In her prayers for her family,
her first thoughts were not for her son and daughter-in-law, but for
the brother who had shielded her from suffering in her widowhood.
Padmavati's sorrow when she overheard the conversation from the
kitchen defies description. Imagine a drowning man thrashing about

in the ocean, expecting imminent death and gulping briny water with each engulfing wave, who looks around desperately for some flotsam for support but is suddenly snatched by a crocodile and pulled under. Such was Padmavati's condition. She sank in an ocean of despair. Once the initial shock wore off, it occurred to Narayanan that the plan he'd worked out for his wife was now ruled out. It was not possible to send her to her father or to her mother. He was afraid he might have to spend his entire life with her and thought he might have to kill her, or make public her shame and cast her aside, or run away himself. He did not have the heart to write to his uncle and add to his suffering.

The tuition would go on till nine and sometimes it was past ten when he returned home to sleep on the thinnai.

It has already been said that Narayanan's expenses increased after separating from Gopalan. Apart from the increase in rent and miscellaneous expenses, he had to buy some essential books for himself. The stipend he received from the college was not enough to cover even a part of these expenses. The meagre savings that Seethai Ammal had managed from her own hard earned income had been used up in the move to Madras. With help from his father-in-law no longer possible, Narayanan began to consider means of augmenting his income. Seethai Ammal wanted to work as before, but Narayanan opposed the idea. He felt it would be very wrong for him, now a responsible adult, married and studying for a BA degree to allow his elderly mother and young wife to earn by cooking for youths like him and selling homemade snacks. This would give room for such youths to refer to him as The son of the Club Woman or The Snack Shop Woman's son. It would also entail occasions when his wife would have to speak to such men, and some undesirable elements among them could misbehave with her, making suggestive gestures or passing cheeky remarks. Rather than permit such a situation, that too when he was over twenty, he felt it would be far better to abandon his studies and work as a coolie, which would earn him enough to support his family and also send a small amount to his uncle.

With this determination, as a first step Narayanan set about effecting economies. He moved out of the house for which he was paying a rent of seven rupees to a poky little two-roomed house on a rent of two rupees. Despite his mother's repeated pleas, he gave up his morning coffee and the glass of milk at night. He was used to nourishment five times a day, including small snacks and main meals. He now reduced this to just two. Padmavati wanted to do likewise, but out of respect for her mother-in-law's feelings, ate thrice a day. Because of his mental anguish, Narayanan could not eat much even at his two meals, which made his mother and wife suspect he was doing so deliberately to reduce expenditure. Despite these measures, Narayanan's budget showed a monthly deficit of over ten rupees. He wanted to bridge this gap somehow without giving up his studies, and pondered over the problem making many enquiries. Finally, he heard of a certain rich gentleman who was willing to pay five rupees per month, for someone to tutor three boys, from six to nine every evening. He met the gentleman and explained his difficulties. The gentleman was impressed with his intelligence and behaviour and, sympathetic of his condition, offered to pay him seven rupees provided he was satisfactory, whereas the previous tutor had been paid only five. Narayanan started on the job. He took to eating supper at five in the evening and then walking to the house of the gentleman two miles away. The tuition would go on till nine, and sometimes it was past ten when he returned home, to sleep on the thinnai. More often he stayed on at the home of his pupils, studying by their light for two or three hours after nine, and then sleeping there. He was in the college library much of the daytime, spending very little time at home, and hardly speaking to anyone. Padmavati tried desperately for an opportunity to talk to him at some length and plead her innocence. But he allowed no scope. Both Padmavati and Seethai Ammal withered in distress day by day, like crops awaiting the monsoon.

Considering his condition, Narayanan's employer gave him his first month's salary in advance. Narayanan gave it to his mother, telling her she would have to manage the entire month with that amount, and the small balance on hand. After repeated careful calculations, that good lady knew this was impossible but was reluctant to tell her son. She restricted her purchases to the minimum of absolute essentials and exercised the strictest economy. To cut expenses, she began observing each of the fasts strict tradition prescribes for women. Thus, she ate nothing on Sunday nights, throughout Monday, as well as on the nights of Friday and Saturday. Apart from this, she starved on the nights of chathurthi, sashti, dasami and amavasai as well as throughout ekadesi. She urged her son and pregnant daughter-in-law to eat well. At the same time, she began to observe fasts even on the days that were not Special. Her object was to somehow manage the household with the amount given by her son, and on no account let any mention of shortage reach his ears. Padmavati knew this well, and ignoring even the needs of the child in her womb, she too began to starve, giving excuses such as loss of appetite, lying about having eaten while her mother-in-law was out, suppressing painful stabs of hunger. The sickness accompanying pregnancy helped her. She couldn't bear to see her mother-in-law's increasing debility and considered it her duty to tell her husband, so that he might think of a way out. She looked through the accounts when Seethai Ammal was out and found that the month's shortfall amounted to two rupees. She told her husband about his mother's attempt to reduce expenditure with frequent fasting. Narayanan, deeply affected by this, wiped the tears from his eyes and went out. That evening he gave three rupees to his mother but evaded an answer when asked how he came by it. Padmavati was puzzled. How was the money produced so soon? She recalled that Narayanan had taken some books with him when going out. She looked through his bookshelf after he left and was startled to find that the two volumes of *Kamba Ramayanam*, a prize given to him by the Hindu College for excellence in Tamil in the FA examination, were missing. She knew what these books meant to him. Apart from the fact that they were given in recognition of merit, there was his intense fascination for Kamban, his pride in the quality of the marginal notes that he had made in the book, the delight he took in reciting and explaining parts of the text, his ecstasy over the beauty of the poetry, leading him at times to kiss the book and make statements like he loved Kamban more than anyone else on earth, his family included, and that even heaven was not worthwhile if there was no Kamban in it. That he should have been driven to disposing these cherished books shattered Padmavati. She felt she had to do something to ease the strain, thought long and hard and decided on a course of action.

So she decided to dispose of two pieces of her
jewellery, murugu and japamalai, which Narayanan
particularly despised.

The vacation was over and the college reopened. Narayanan secured third rank and went on to the next class. Gopalan, however, was the last in the class, and was detained. As he had not been able to meet Narayanan before leaving for home, Gopalan wrote two or three letters to him, giving news about the situation at home and the division of their family property. But there was no reply. Gopalan wrote at the close of the vacation, giving the date of his return to Madras and asking Narayanan to meet him at the station. This too was ignored.

Padmavati's idea for easing their financial stringency was to convert some of her jewellery into cash by pledging or selling it. Generally, women are extremely fond of jewellery and Padmavati's love of ornaments was rather more than average. But understanding her husband's aversion to jewellery, she tried, with some success, to overcome this inclination. So, she wore only the jewels considered bare essentials. The rest, pieces she had cajoled or bullied her father into buying, were locked up. Now, in their struggle for sheer existence she thought it ridiculous, like looking for ghee with butter in hand, to let these assets lie idle in her trunk. She estimated that over and above what her husband got by way of stipend and tuition salary, a hundred rupees would take care of all the household and educational expenses for the year that remained of his BA course. So she decided to dispose of two pieces of her jewellery, the murugu and japamalai, which Narayanan particularly despised. She was well aware that her mother-in-law would never accept this, so strong was her principle that whatever was brought in by the daughter-in-law of the house should never be exchanged or sold. But Narayanan had no such inhibitions. He himself could be asked to make the sale, but he was not on talking terms. She imagined that presenting him with the money unexpectedly might bring about a change of heart. He might note her great concern and understand that her love was deep and true. He might even appease his mother's distress over her action. Thus, Padmavati felt, the selling of jewellery could achieve two cherished objectives, provide an antidote for the pain of poverty, and redeem the lost love of her husband. Nonetheless, some doubts still lingered in her mind and she hesitated to act.

Meanwhile, with the reopening of the college, Narayanan's condition became worse. He did not eat anything until his morning meal at ten, before going to college. He did not come home in the afternoon or eat anything. His classes, which went on until five, did not give him much time before his tuition, and he went straight from the college to his pupils' house. His next meal was only at ten the following morning. This made Seethai Ammal also increase her fasts. After this had gone on for two or three days Padmavati, distressed by the clear evidence of hunger and starvation in their appearance, decided to act on her idea regardless of the consequences. She arranged for the secret sale of her murugu and japamalai through her friend and nextdoor neighbour Valliammai, a chettiar woman.

Narayanan did not teach on Sundays, and on those evenings he went to the beach and spent a long time there, lost in thought. On the Sunday that followed the college reopening, he picked up a book and left for the beach at four o'clock. But he was unable to read anything, haunted by thoughts of his plight. Finally, unable to stand the tension, he rose and walked away aimlessly hoping to suppress his bitterness. After a while, he found he was walking in the direction of his house and not wanting to retrace his steps, decided on going home. As he turned the corner of the lane, he saw Gopalan come out of his house and walk in his direction but without noticing him. He immediately recalled Gopalan's letter received a few days earlier, telling him of his planned arrival that morning. To avoid meeting him he turned round and entered a bylane, hurrying home after Gopalan had passed by. The front door was bolted from inside. As he neared he heard Padmavati's happy voice singing *Ee diname su dinamu*. From the bolted door and Padmavati's singing, Narayanan concluded that his mother was not at home. He surmised that Padmavati's joyous exuberance, at a time when he and his mother were steeped in misery, followed from Gopalan's visit. His fury knew no bounds and he banged on the door. Padmavati stopped singing and opened the door thinking that it was her mother-in-law returning from the temple. But encountering her husband, his face ablaze with rage, she was slightly startled and stood aside silent and diffident. This only strengthened Narayanan's suspicion.

"Where is Amma?"

"She has gone to the temple," replied Padmavati. "She left soon after you. I thought it was she knocking on the door."

"Why did that fellow come here? With whom was he talking?"

Padmavati was puzzled. "Which fellow? No one came here. I was singing because I had some good news."

"What good news?"

Padmavati took out a purse tucked in her hip and gave it to Narayanan. "Look at this. There are a hundred rupees here. We don't have to struggle anymore. This'll do for the whole year."

"How did you get this?"

"Come on," started Padmavati jocularly. "Let's see if you can guess. What'll you give me if I tell you?"

But seeing Narayanan's rising anger, she was scared.

"No … don't be angry, please. I didn't steal or gamble or sell myself. I only sold the murugu and japamalai that you always hated. That's how I got the money."

"When did Gopalan come here?"

"Gopalan? You mean Gopalanna? Has he come back? Has Kalyani Manni come too? He didn't come here."

"Padmi, listen carefully." Narayanan bolted the front door and continued. "Hitherto I had only suspicions, but today I saw for myself. You cannot dupe me any longer. Just own up and tell me everything. You've no idea of my anger. If you try to hide even an iota of the truth, I'll kill you this minute. With this disgrace, life is of no importance. Tell me, when did that traitor, that wretched, treacherous rascal come here? Did he give you only this money or anything else? Tell me everything."

Padmavati was devastated. Trembling and incoherent, she said, "Oh, how unjust! I only know that I wanted to relieve our suffering. I couldn't bear to see the way you struggle, going without proper food. I knew Amma wouldn't agree, and so asked my friend Valliammai to sell the murugu and japamalai. I got these hundred rupees from her just now after Amma left. I thought that if I gave it to you as a surprise you'd be pleased, that it would end your suspicions, and you'd know of my innocence and deep love and respect for you. You'd always made fun of those jewels, saying they made me look like a gypsy and a Muslim. I thought that by getting rid of them, good times would return. I know nothing else. I wasn't even aware that Gopalanna had returned. Please ask Amma to find out the truth about the jewels from Valliammai. Look inside my trunk and see if the jewels are there. Forget your suspicions and take the money."

Narayanan threw the purse on her face. "You betray me and then try to thrust the charity of your paramour on me, you wretch! And who's this Valliammai, another whore like you? Is she also his keep? And *she* is your witness! Tell me the truth or I'll kill you."

He pulled her by the hair and heaping unprintable abuses, hit her, pushed her down and kicked her two or three times. Padmavati fainted. Narayanan left her in that condition, opened the door and sat on the thinnai in a daze, like a man who had lost his senses. It was quite some time before Padmavati regained consciousness. She was unable to get up, and felt as if a wrench was working away at the pit of her stomach. She lay with tears streaming down her face, suffering the steadily rising pain in silence, teeth clenched. Returning home, Seethai Ammal saw her distraught son on the thinnai and asked him what the matter was. He did not answer and she went in. Shocked by Padmavati's condition, she questioned her. But Padmavati only said that she was lying down and weeping because her stomach was aching, and that nothing had happened. Seethai Ammal tried all the home remedies known to her, but to no avail. That night, Padmavati lost the child she was carrying.

The doctor came twice a day to see Padmavati, who was suffering acutely, hovering between life and death.

P admavati's agony following the unhappy events recorded in the previous chapter constitutes a tale of intense woe. For the first two days, Narayanan was completely indifferent. But his mother was very worried and expressed her anxiety constantly. He was troubled, first by the feeling that it was not right to ignore the illness of anyone even if she was an unfaithful wife and also by the trace of affection that still lingered, despite all that had happened. Hence he decided to seek medical assistance. Seethai Ammal knew from experience that only English Medicine could help in her daughter-in-law's condition and advised her son to get a good doctor, regardless of expense, resorting to sale of jewellery if necessary. She did not know anything about what had taken place between her son and daughter-in-law and thought Padmavati's miscarriage had come about through natural causes. Narayanan, however, knew it was a consequence of his brutality, and understood the seriousness of the life threatening condition. The thought that her death could be a solution to his problems crossed his mind fleetingly in moments of despair. But he was well aware that the responsibility for such a death would be his, legally and morally. He was horrified by the possibility. Consultation with a good doctor would cost him fifty or sixty rupees and he did not possess even that many annas. There was no scope for borrowing. His mother's suggestion of sale of jewellery was also not acceptable. Caring for a sick wife, even an unfaithful one, was a husband's duty and selling her jewellery for that purpose was to him extremely degrading. Nor could he consider using the hundred rupees she swore she got through sale of the jewels and he believed had been gifted by her paramour. After thinking deeply over all these alternatives, he finally approached Dr Miller, explaining his own poverty and the urgency for medical assistance. That gentleman was concerned, and immediately despatched a note to his personal physician through his servant. Within two hours, the distinguished doctor called at Narayanan's house and examined Padmavati. He suspected that the miscarriage had not come about through natural causes and questioned Padmavati gently and tactfully. But she insisted that apart from an accidental fall near the tap, nothing untoward had happened. How could she, who had made no mention of her husband's cruelty even to the mother-in-law who cared for her more than a mother, talk about it to the doctor? He then questioned Narayanan closely in English, at first gently and then with veiled threats, but he insisted that nothing had happened. He really wished to confess to the doctor, but could hardly tell him the true reasons for the quarrel. And he also knew that if the doctor were to come to know that he had kicked and beaten a woman, that too in this condition, he would incur his scorn and revulsion. He wondered if it was the fear of punishment for his crime that had prevented him from telling the truth and felt very uncomfortable. However, he soon consoled himself with the thought that this was not so.

The doctor came twice a day to see Padmavati, who was suffering acutely, hovering between life and death. She prayed constantly for deliverance through death. With the loss of the one dear hope that had sustained her all along, her forbearance ended. She had borne her husband's cruelty with fortitude because of the child she was carrying, a symbol of their brief, happy life together. Even in her third month of pregnancy, she felt sure that the baby would be a boy and in her imaginings, she had named it, fondled it and seen in its features a reflection of her husband's. She had hoped to regain her husband's lost love through the child. She had made little dresses, caps, socks and beaded ornaments to adorn the child. But now all the sweet plans of her childlike heart had vanished like a passing dream. When the man she loved and revered hated her, she saw no point in sustaining life. If her death would give her husband some happiness, she felt somehow she should abandon life and fulfil her pativrata dharma. The effect of the expert medical treatment was much reduced by this psychological factor. She did not heed the doctor's orders of complete bed rest, nor did she take the prescribed medications regularly.

Seethai Ammal was steeped in sorrow. The difficulties of her brother, of her own household and the rift between her son and daughter-in-law pained her very much. She had been eagerly looking forward to the birth of a grandson. The loss of that hope stretched her endurance almost beyond limit. She knew from personal experience the immense suffering caused by abortions, and also knew that they made future pregnancies difficult. Her only thought now was that her daughter-in-law should live. She began to feel that all the misfortunes of her family were because of her, as she was predestined to suffer and witness suffering. This led to the thought that with her death, happiness would return to her loved ones. She began to pray to Yamadharmaraja and other gods to take her life instead of her daughter-in-law's. This idea, once occurred, took firm root in her mind and grew swiftly to become an obsession.

On ekadesi, some ten days after Padmavati's illness, Seethai Ammal told her son, "Nanu, don't go to college today. Don't leave the house. I'll die by tonight. Don't leave my side."

The sincerity of her tone and clarity of expression startled Narayanan. But he turned it into a joke. "Amma, you always said you didn't want to die in Patnam because a pariah would touch your body in the cremation ground. You wanted to die only in our village. Shall we take the train this evening?"

"All that is foolish belief," Seethai Ammal said. "As you used to say, Nothing matters in death. Don't borrow or waste money on my obsequies. Just listen carefully to the mantras recited by the priest and repeat them correctly. That'll do. To the best of my knowledge, I've done no wrong. It is for god to decide whether it is heaven or hell for me. Treat this child Padmi kindly at least hereafter. She would never have wilfully caused you harm. And she will not do so in future. Remember she has no one apart from you, and you have no one other than her."

Padmavati cut in, "Why should you die, Amma? My death would end my troubles and perhaps give relief to your son. I'm of no use to anyone. Your help and kindness are needed by all."

"Padmi, you're very young. You are of the rising generation with a life ahead and should not utter such words. You have to bear children and live happily. Your present distress makes you talk like this. Don't lose heart. Suffering is common to every soul born on this earth. Is our lot worse than that of Sita Devi, Damayanti or Chandramati? How can any mortal, who has heard of Sri Rama's suffering even mention that word? One appreciates the shade only when one has been in the sun. It's my wretched presence that is causing you distress. Everything will be well once I go. Wait and watch. Your deliverance begins tomorrow. Later, you'll recall what I've said."

"Amma, you seem determined to die," said Narayanan continuing in the same light vein. "Are you going to consume poison? Remember, that might perhaps land us in prison. Or has your ekadesi fast affected you?"

"Death by suicide is bad and will lead to hell. As for fasting, I've done so much of it that it has nothing to do with what I say. I'm sure to die today and Padmi will begin to improve right away. My prayers have been heeded. Don't think I'm joking. Last night I dreamt that your father came in a vimanam and asked me to get in beside him. That will never prove false."

"Is that all?" laughed Narayanan. "I thought it was something more serious. Well, you may die in your dream!"

Despite all his pleas and arguments, she did not let him go to college that day. Unable to refuse her, he stayed at home and studied. After her bath and prayer, Seethai Ammal went to the temple for darshanam, something she never did in the mornings. Then she cooked and served a meal to her son and daughter-in-law but ate nothing herself. She sat in prayer, uttering the name of Rama, with vibhuti smeared on her forehead and body, rudraksha in hand, the embodiment of piety.

At around four, Seethai Ammal suddenly cried, "Padmi! Narayana!" It was like Gajendra's cry, when caught by a crocodile. Before Narayanan and his wife could reach her, she had lost speech. She made them sit on either side, and taking Padmavati's hands, placed them in Narayanan's and looked from one to the other repeatedly, with a mixture of love, sorrow, compassion and supplication in her eyes. How could anyone possibly interpret that look now? It was never to be forgotten by Narayanan or his wife and continued to haunt them always. Soon Seethai Ammal's sight dimmed, and her head drooped. Narayanan began to tremble and lifting her up gently placed her head on his right thigh, while his wife placed the feet on her lap. There was a small sound, a gentle "Ku," perhaps the sound of the gates of heaven opening to admit Seethai Ammal's soul. Narayanan and his wife sat for a long while with the body on their laps, bathing it with their tears.

If totally alone she would try to avoid fear by busying
herself reading or singing and keep to the front thinnai
or the passage.

Narayanan sent a telegram to his uncle but he didn't come. Seethai Ammal's obsequies were done according to her wish, without much expense and in keeping with the requirements of the sastras. Savithri stayed in the house for the first few days to give company to poor Padmavati, sick and bereft of support. Some of Seethai Ammal's friends also dropped in now and then. Gopalan came a couple of times, tried to offer consolation to Narayanan, offered money for expenses and asked him the reason why he was offended with him. But since Narayanan gave no proper reply and his face clearly reflected his bitterness and resentment, Gopalan kept away. Narayanan did not talk much with Savithri, but her mere presence and occasional conversation soothed him and gave him some peace of mind. But, after a few days, Savithri went back.

Staying alone with his wife increased Narayanan's misery. He never spoke to her and spent the greater part of the day at the college or at the gentleman's house. Occasionally, the thought of his young, childlike wife, all alone behind the locked doors of the house like a prisoner behind bars, crossed his mind and he felt a stab of pity for her. He felt that this sad lot had befallen her only because she had married him. But at other times, when he imagined that his faithless friend and wretched wife might be amorously engaged, he would burn with fury. When such thoughts took hold, no matter where he was and what he was doing, he would immediately drop everything and rush home, only to find nothing more than a closed door. Even the slightest sign of happiness on Gopalan's face or his wife's drove him to a frenzy. For one reason or the other, he would sometimes physically assault Padmavati and be cruel to her. Some days the thought that he was being rather foolish did cross his mind, and he would then feel sorry for his wife and show her some consideration, though there was no return of the old love. Altogether, he was subject to such quick changes of mood and his behaviour was so erratic that any observer would promptly have termed him crazy.

Poor, unfortunate Padmavati! Words cannot adequately describe her woe. Born and brought up in a large household in a village and raised with love and care, she was used to always having people around her. By nature, she dreaded being alone. When her husband and mother-in-law both happened to be out she would get her neighbour, Valliammai, to keep her company. If totally alone, she would try to avoid fear by busying herself reading or singing, and keep to the front thinnai or the passage. At night, even if the house was full of people, she would never enter a room without a light. If she had to pass through a dark, unlighted area alone, she would close her eyes tight and run through. Such fears did not lessen as she grew older and Narayanan used to tease her about it. A night light was kept burning for her in the bedroom. All the spooky stories she had heard would overwhelm her if she chanced to wake up at night.

Now fate decreed that she should be alone all the time. It was at her request that Savithri spent some days with her. After her departure, she had no company. She dropped Valliammai's friendship following Narayanan's cruel remarks on the day the jewellery was sold. Narayanan would be at home, studying until ten in the morning. He then left after a meal, to return only at nine, after his evening tuition. Padmavati spent the intervening hours all alone behind a bolted door, day after day. What thoughts would have assailed her mind then? What fears haunted her? She would tremble at the idea of ghosts. Terror would strike her heart when she thought of the possibility of some villains scaling the backyard wall and forcing their way into the house to molest her. How was she to keep these terrible thoughts in check? Reading was possible, but how much could she read and for how long? Would her eyes not tire? Music was hardly possible, for how could she sing without any joy in her heart? Sleep was absolutely impossible. Thoughts of suicide occurred very often, and she came close to it but stopped, because she realized her husband would be left alone without anyone even to provide him food. There was also this small, lingering spark of hope that one day she would regain her husband's love. Is human life possible without this eternal spring of hope?

Padmavati spent the greater part of her lonely days in housework and study. Cleaning the house and cooking took up the mornings. Like her husband, she too ate nothing in the mornings. She served him his meal when he finished his bath, bolted the door after he left for college and then ate. Next came the task of washing the vessels and used clothes and mending them if necessary, attending to odd jobs and dusting and cleaning her husband's study. By then it would be around two o'clock and Padmavati would take up her Tamil books. With Narayanan not on talking terms, there was no scope for help and guidance, but she tried to proceed with the help of a dictionary for difficult words. She also used this time to learn the *Kural* by heart. At five in the evening, she would once again clean the house and start the night meal, spread her husband's bed and light a lamp in his room. The hours between seven and nine at night were the worst for her, spent awaiting her husband's return. When he did come, he would eat and then immediately go into his room. She would then finish her own meal and the cleaning up and lie down in the kitchen with the light of a little lamp and her tears for company.

Ever since suspicion took root in Narayanan's mind, even while Seethai Ammal was alive, she had begun to sleep in the kitchen. Earlier Seethai Ammal was with her but after her death, Padmavati was all alone.

During this time, Padmavati began to record her thoughts and daily events in a notebook. Although her intention was mainly to pass time, she did sometimes feel that if and when good times returned, she could derive some satisfaction from looking back on all that she had endured. Here is a sample of entries.

Monday: What is there to write day after day? But I've never suffered as I did today. After Athaan left for college, I finished the household chores and went into his room. While I was arranging his books, a letter dropped down. It was a letter Athaan had once written to me. Recollections of the past choked me as I read it, making me almost sob aloud. I did weep for a while. But whether I weep or laugh, I have no one but myself for company. Sita Devi was better off in her captivity as she had her keepers, horrible rakshasis though they were, for company. But I don't have even that solace, someone to whom I can voice my misery. While I was immersed in these thoughts, I heard a thud in the back veranda. It sounded as if a snake had dropped from the roof, and I was very scared. What was I to do if it really was a snake? If I locked myself in the room, I wouldn't know its movements and I would have to go and open the door for Athaan. The thought then occurred that death by snakebite would be a way of release. I steadied my fluttering heart and peeped out and saw two squirrels chasing each other in love-play. The joy these small creatures share is denied to me. Athaan and I no longer have that love and companionship and we both suffer torment. How long is this to go on? If someone were to tell me with certainty that my

Athaan and I would be happy together again after ten years, I think I can spend the time till then crossing off each passing day. But this uncertainty is intolerable. O Swami, Parvatipanga, Lakshminarayana, give me the patience and strength to bear my lot, that is my prayer, my supplication.

Friday: How can I describe the terror I felt at the thunder and lightning that flashed today. I could never bear the sound of thunder and always had to hug someone, Ammami, Athai or Athaan, nearby. But today I could do nothing else but hug the pillow and lie face down, my eyes tightly closed. I thought that Athaan, who was aware of my fears, would say something when he came home. But he ate his food silently and went to his room. After a while, I heard his voice and peeped in eagerly thinking he had called me. But no, he was merely reading aloud from a book. I felt so sad that I just couldn't control my tears. Because he had coughed a little while eating, I prepared a kashayam of athimaduram and offered it to him saying, Athaan, take this, you have a cough. He looked up, stared at me and then swept aside the glass. Ayyo, how can I describe my sorrow? Did he think that I was perhaps trying to poison him? I long for a word from him, spoken even in anger. I don't dare speak to him. I couldn't sleep a wink, as horrible thoughts crowded my mind. Why did Brahma make me a woman? Of what earthly use am I? Is there deliverance in store for me? God alone knows.

Saturday: I don't know whose was the first face I saw today, but that's a face I'd like to see every day. As always, I was immersed in misery when suddenly I felt that I had the strength to put an end to my life. I was knotting a rope when I heard a knock on the door. I threw the rope aside and called, Who is it? It's me, said Athaan and knocked again. When I opened the door, he came in and stood for a few minutes, looking confused. He asked, Padmi, what were you doing? I didn't have the courage to tell the truth and said, Nothing. I was just lying down. He then picked up a book and left without saying anything more. The fact that he came, so unusually, and that too when I was planning death as if to stop my suicide, indicates beyond doubt that our relationship is to continue. God in His infinite love sent him at that time. For me, to attempt suicide again would be an act of betrayal. And he called me "Padmi!" That one word is enough to keep me happy for a month. How true is the saying that one appreciates the shade only after being in the sun! In the past, when he kept calling me Padmi! Padmi! repeatedly, it sometimes embarrassed and sometimes irritated me. But now it sounds heavenly. Perhaps he came to see me, feeling sorry for my loneliness. Otherwise, there's no reason for his coming home during class hours. Hope has sprung in my mind that by somehow living through this, I can again be as before. What is god's will, who knows?

Narayanan rushed in to gather up in his arms the beloved he had not touched for some months.

It has already been said that Narayanan did experience despair and disgust at his own state of mind. When his wife's infidelity seemed established beyond doubt, he blamed himself for not killing her like Othello and deprecated his faint heart. The memory of the bliss that had once been his persisted stubbornly, and revealed his abiding love for his wife, just as the presence of the jathimalli, the jasmine, locked up securely in a box, is revealed by its escaping fragrance. He was determined that this memory should somehow be eradicated and that he should take revenge by killing his wife. At other times, he asked himself how falsehood could coexist with so much beauty and love. Despite all these contrary thoughts, he remained convinced of his wife's guilt. Unable to withstand the mental turmoil, he sought solitude at the beach one Sunday evening, hoping to reach some decision. He went over the whole situation in his mind and decided that his wife was indeed guilty. To his jaundiced eye, the evidence seemed conclusive. Since she was guilty, he started thinking about his future course of action. This seemed unending. He was able to see clearly that his present behaviour was unjust and inappropriate. But what else could he do? He recalled Tennyson's lines about the evil effects that would follow when a husband permitted his unfaithful wife to continue to live in his household and felt that on no account should he and Padmavati live under the same roof. But what was he to do? Sending her back to his uncle's house was not possible as sunk in penury both he and his wife were at different places. It also seemed contrary to his marriage contract that he, who had lived with their daughter as long as it suited his pleasure, should send her back when she caused him distress. The alternative was to kill her. But the very thought was abhorrent. How could he touch that beautiful body and destroy it?

The confusion of contradictory emotions drove him to a frenzy. He tore at his hair, struck his face repeatedly and sobbed loudly. This outburst calmed him slightly, and again it seemed to him that he had to kill Padmavati. At that very moment, in a flash, he saw his mother on her deathbed placing Padmavati's hands in his and looking pleadingly at both of them. How strange! All his blind fury and cruel intent melted like wax. He could only remember the ardour and matchless joy of his close companionship with Padmavati. He recalled that he had once sat with her at that very spot in intimate conversation. He remembered their mutual promises, the frank and open revelations of their secret thoughts and desires and their joy over the similarity of these. He felt that if only there could be even a momentary return of that mutual bliss, they could both walk to death into the sea, without the slightest regret. His thoughts could proceed no further. Wiping his tears he rose and slowly reciting doleful English poems, began to walk homewards.

When Narayanan reached home, the front door was closed as usual. But he did not push it open and sat on the thinnai as he heard Padmavati singing in a soft voice that could melt the heart of a stone, "O Lord, when O Lord will you take pity on me? I'm innocent, unaware of wrong. You are my succour. I have no refuge but you." This, sung with intense feeling, touched the core of Narayanan's heart and his eyes streamed. Before he could steady himself, Padmavati went on in a soulful voice reflecting her inner anguish, "How can I bear my lot? O Lord!" This plaint pierced Narayanan's heart like a red hot iron passing through butter. At this point she stopped singing and cried, "Adiamma, I can't stand it anymore," and fainted. As if in a frenzy, Narayanan pushed open the door, and rushed in to gather up in his arms the beloved he had not touched for some months.

Finally he took the first letter from his pocket and silently gave it to Gopalan who read it with obvious signs of embarrassment.

While the events in the previous chapter were happening, the following conversation was taking place between Gopalan and Savithri. As usual, Gopalan was about to set out for Shala's house on the pretext of going out for a stroll. Savithri stopped him and asked him to stay and talk to her as she was feeling listless and depressed. Gopalan could not refuse her request.

"What is wrong, Akka, why are you depressed?" Gopalan asked. "You've never talked like this before. Are you finding it difficult to stay at home all by yourself?"

"It's not that at all. I don't need any company and I can't complain about it. I was thinking of Padmavati's plight. Nanu, like you, is away at college during the day. And then he doesn't get back until ten at night. That poor girl, she is just a child, has to be all by herself. When they were here, she used to be scared of going into the kitchen alone. I can't imagine how she's managing now. Even while he's at home, it seems Nanu doesn't talk to her. I feel that even my lot is better than hers! You don't know how sorry I am for her. You've told me not to go to their house often. I never dreamt that you and Nanu could drift apart like this."

"He's so adamant, how can I help it? How much can one tolerate for the sake of friendship? Once, twice, ten times! But can one give up self-respect altogether? You know the whole thing. He left our house because of that wretched Sangu's mischief. Even that wasn't really necessary, but perhaps it was justified. Why should that affect our friendship? Why should he insult me? I put up with his temper. I've written so many letters and tried to talk to him so often. What can I do when I'm always rudely brushed aside for no reason? In spite of that, we did try our best to help when Seethai Ammal died, but he refused to allow even that. Well, let him simmer in his own anger. For any failing on our part, we can make amends, but that's not the problem. If he chooses enmity for no reason, what can we do?"

Savithri was thoughtful. "But Gopu, Nanu's not a casual friend. We know him so well. There must be some explanation for his behaviour. He will not act like this without reason. And then ..."

"What possible reason can there be, tell me?" cut in Gopalan. "Sangu is no longer with us. And it's not with us alone that his behaviour is strange. You say that he doesn't talk to his wife. I wonder if something is wrong with his mind. I believe he sometimes leaves the classroom suddenly, in the middle of a lesson. One day ..."

At this point, Narayanan burst into the house. Astonished, they merely stood up in silence. He turned to Gopalan, "Gopu, I want to talk with you in private. Please come to the beach."

Gopalan was a little nervous about going out alone with Narayanan and glanced at Savithri. But her face showed no reservation. The two of them walked in silence and reaching the beach sat down on the sands. Narayanan attempted to say something a couple of times but words seemed to fail him. Finally he took the first letter from his pocket and silently gave it to Gopalan, who read it with obvious signs of embarrassment.

Sighing deeply he said, "How did this reach your hands?"

Wordlessly Narayanan gave him the envelope.

Shocked, Gopalan said, "This is an awful trick played by someone. I wrote this letter to Shala ... you know, wife of Nagamier, the Canal Superintendent of our town. You may remember the incident in the passage of our house. She's now here, in Mannadi. I don't have to hide this from you, she's my keep now. I wrote this to her in the early days of our relationship."

Even as he spoke, Narayanan gave him the second letter. Glancing at it Gopalan said, "This is not my writing. Oh, what a diabolic plan! I know, I'm sure this is the work of that wretched brother of mine. Sangu got the first letter from Shala and after sending it in a new cover, composed a second one to strengthen his plot. Ada paavi, what a rogue! And he, my brother! Look Nanu, look at this first letter. See how the paper below my signature has been torn off. I'd written a verse on Shala, with her name in it. He knew that couldn't stand, and removed it. Blackguard, look how cleverly he has forged my writing!"

Narayanan was stunned and speechless. With all his doubts vanishing in a trice, he was overcome with shame for allowing himself to be duped so easily. Greater still was his remorse over the harsh treatment of his boyhood friend and the heartless cruelty to his loving wife even when she was pregnant. He put his arms around Gopalan's neck and wept on his shoulder. Gopalan too could not control his tears. After talking it over further, Narayanan assured Gopalan that all his misgivings had vanished and repeatedly begged forgiveness. But Gopalan insisted on giving further proof and virtually dragged Narayanan to Shala's house. Shala did not recognize Narayanan and Gopalan merely said he was one of his friends. He then cleverly brought the conversation round to the letter he had written to her and asked Shala to bring it. She made a pretence of looking for it and said it was probably mislaid. But Gopalan insisted on an explanation, and feigning anger asked her to think again and tell him. Finally she admitted to having given it to Iyengar and said that when she had asked for it, he told her that Sangu had lost it. Gopalan then produced the letter and Shala said it was indeed the letter she had received and on her own added that the poem at the end had been torn off.

Now with everything clear as daylight, the joyous relief of the friends more than made up for their earlier distress. They could not reveal the whole story to Savithri because of Shala's involvement. But they did say that the misunderstanding was on account of a letter Sangu had forged, that everything had been explained and that they were firmer friends than ever before. For Savithri, the joy of their reunion was overshadowed by the pain caused by Sangu's behaviour.

Do we need to record here that our heroine did not sleep in the kitchen that night?

Gopalan, greatly pleased, took a week's leave from college
and went to his wife's village.

As soon as Narayanan was relieved of one mental tension, he was gripped by another. Once the misunderstanding with Gopalan was cleared, he was troubled by his friend's affair with Shala while his wife and child were away. When he took up the matter with Gopalan the very next day and argued with the old familiarity and concern, he found that Gopalan, brought up with good values, was not entirely comfortable about the relationship. He also came to understand that Savithri was completely in the dark. Gopalan's initial irritation with his wife's behaviour as well as his infatuation with Shala had begun to wane. So Narayanan was able to change his mind through affectionate advice combined with threat of disclosure to Savithri. He also told him that if he would bring back his wife, Narayanan would once again share the same house with him. Gopalan, greatly pleased, took a week's leave from college, left Savithri in Narayanan's house and went to his wife's village.

It was about six in the evening when Gopalan reached his father-in-law's house. His sudden appearance surprised everyone, and when it was known that he had come to take back his wife and child, there was great joy. Needless to say, Pannai Muthier and his wife could never have enough of their darling daughter and grandson. But they could not bear their daughter's distress, though she tried hard to hide it. They had heard about the affairs of their son-in-law, who had left his wife behind on the pretext of studies, and the informant was none other than his own brother. So, understandably, they were immensely relieved and happy.

There are some among us who are insensitive to the feelings of a couple about to be reunited after long separation. They fail to understand the pain of separation and the impatience for the reunion. They take delight in pointless conversation and silly banter. Gopalan, luckily, was spared this. His mother-in-law postponed the mandatory feast for the visiting son-in-law to the next day, served a quick supper and despatched the couple to their bedroom.

There is nothing stranger on earth than the mind of man. Gopalan had a complete change of heart with Narayanan's advice. His fascination for Shala had turned to hatred. His heart now brimmed with love for his child and wife, and he longed for the moment when, after making a full confession and begging her forgiveness, he could overwhelm his wife with his ardour. He who had found the train too slow, who could hardly wait for the moment of reunion, now sat on a chair silent, grave. Could it be that his tongue, which had uttered endearments to Shala, was now too stiff even to call his wife by name? Was it that the arms that had embraced Shala hesitated even to touch his wife? Was it that the eyes that had revelled in Shala's charms were unable to focus on his wife?

Gopalan at least had a reason. But what made Kalyani lie sobbing on her pillow? Was all her earlier display of grief a pretence? When the news of her husband's affair reached her, she spent two or three days in utter despair refusing even to eat. Then she consoled herself that his behaviour had been caused by separation and the natural male instincts. She recollected only the good aspects of his nature and wanted above all to be reunited with him. She prayed to all the gods and made secret vows that he should come back to her, promising herself that she would welcome him with love, place his child at his feet and embracing him tell him of all her sorrow.

As Kalyani's sobs rose in tempo, Gopalan steadied himself, got up and sat beside her on the cot, saying, "Kalyanam, look, I'm here. I'll never leave you again. Don't weep. Do get up." As he tried to turn her face towards him, she recoiled, pushed his hand aside and swiftly moved over to sit on the other side of the cot. "How dare you touch me with the hands that touched Shala? Do you think I'm a prostitute too?" she hissed.

Gopalan was shocked. He did not know that his wife was aware of his misdeed. After all, Savithri who lived with him in the same house did not know of it and this made him feel secure in the belief that distant Kalyani could never hear of it. He had thought of telling her only a part of the truth. It would have upset her, but would have also served to win her full trust. He wondered if he should deny everything. But Kalyani even knew the name! Who could have told her? What else did she know? Could he hide the truth from her? For how long? Is it possible to hide a whole pumpkin in a serving of rice? He concluded that it would be best to somehow put an end to the problem right away.

He was silent for a while and then said, "Kalyanam, do stop crying and listen to me. I'll tell you the truth. I thought you wouldn't have heard, but I did want to confess and seek forgiveness. That is why I came. But you already know ..."

Kalyani cried out, "Aa deivamé, why should I continue to live? I didn't believe what people said. I thought my husband would never have strayed. I asked myself, Why should he desert me? Was I not pretty enough, rich enough? But now he comes, after a relationship with a woman common to thousands ..." She struck her forehead repeatedly and fell face down on the bed. Gopalan became a little nervous. He lifted her gently, placed her on his lap and rocked her, patting her on the back, as if pacifying a child, consoling her with words and phrases we cannot describe here. She kept sobbing for a long while and then gradually quietened. Finally, after his repeated requests, she allowed him to have his say.

Gopalan said, "Kalyanam, if you would only listen to me a little patiently, you won't be so distressed. And you won't think so badly of me either. It is true that I visited Shala. I'm not trying to deny that. I admit it was wrong of me, but the mistake was not entirely mine. Unwittingly, you were a cause. I've told you of the incident involving Shala and me in the passage of our house. Nanu also knows about it. From that you can see that my love for you is true, and I'm not by nature inclined to go astray. I was intoxicated by your beauty, and in my love for you, took no note of your faults. But in course of time they became apparent and I was deeply hurt. Of course everyone has faults, and one sees others' faults more clearly than one's own. You used to fuss terribly over trivial things. Your stubborn tantrums affected my studies. I wanted you to study and come up to my expectations of a good wife. You didn't have the slightest interest in studies. At first I was only saddened, but slowly I began to detest it. You would weep and throw tantrums every night. I began to dread the nights and not look forward to the promise of love like other husbands. I often contemplated killing you and myself. You were a hindrance to my studies and I wanted to be separated from you somehow. It was at that time, as fate would have it, I chanced to meet Shala. The same fate not only decreed that I should be separated from Nanu, but also that I should have some bad elements as friends, all at a time when you were not with me. This combination of circumstances was just my Bad Time. But I swear, believe me, my love for you was never affected and never will be. I can never forget the bliss we've experienced. It was only my desire for that bliss, without your tears and my worries, that drove me astray. Never for a moment did I forget my love for you, nor did I ever believe her words of love. I acted very wrongly, like someone setting fire to his home to get rid of rats. Now I've regained Nanu's friendship and given up bad company. I have come to you with more love than ever before, like one seeking shade after being in the sun. Keeping me from straying again is your responsibility. Forgive me and forget everything." Gopalan spoke softly, with sincerity and humility.

Kalyani sat silently, chin in hand, for a long while. Finally she sighed and her tears started flowing again. "Hold me tight, I am choking. I feel strange," she buried her face in his chest and wept out her misery.

The next night Kalyani said, "Adé yogya, you were so honest, you argued so well yesterday, and finally made everything seem my fault. And I accepted that. But tell me now. If there were some faults in you that made me go to another man, would you have accepted that? Again, suppose Padmavati had behaved like me, would your friend have sought Shala?"

Gopalan's conscience was pricked by both the questions. Narayanan had not strayed, even when he believed his wife was unfaithful. While he was steeped in thought, Kalyani said playfully, "No reply? What's sealing your mouth, Oi? Can't be Kozhukkattai. Today's not Vinayaka Chathurthi."

"I've already told you that I've erred badly. It hurts me if you refer to it again and again. Don't torture me. Didn't we promise yesterday to forget the past?"

"Ammanji, I'm sorry, I spoke without thinking. Excuse me this last time. If I ever refer to it again, throw tantrums without reason or not act according to your wishes in studies and other things to the extent I can, you may seek not one but a thousand Shalas. I swear that as a chaste woman I shall fulfil this promise."

Seeing the students who cluster around him clamouring "Saar! Saar!" it does look like his ambition is being fulfilled.

T hree years have passed. Our friends still live in Patnam, in two adjoining houses.

Narayanan passed his BA securing a first class. With the help of his Principal, he got a job in a school on a salary of seventy rupees and studied privately for his MA. He got a first class in MA also, and is now teaching on a salary of one hundred and fifty rupees. His pride and joy at being a teacher is immense. His aim is to be like Rajagopala Iyer, his old teacher at Irangal, a guide to his pupils not only in studies, but in the principles of life as well. Seeing the students who cluster around him in the evenings clamouring, "Saar! Saar!" it does look like his ambition is being fulfilled. He has developed a new habit after reading some books on physical fitness. He spends at least two hours a day playing ball or doing exercises and advises everyone close to him to do likewise. From Padmavati's trim and beautiful figure, it does seem that this practice is good for women too. Narayanan's uncle and aunt are living with him. As soon as he got a job, Narayanan went over to settle the matter of his uncle's debts, and arranged for a monthly remittance towards the repayment of the loans. That payment is still going on, but it is said that the debts will be fully cleared in a year.

Our heroine Padmavati has a child, a son who never leaves her side, and who bears a remarkable likeness to Narayanan. She has achieved Pandit status in Tamil and in private, converses with her husband in English. It would seem that she might begin to write poetry in English very soon. She is also learning the veena and vocal music. To people who express surprise at her progress, she recites the kural which says that hard work can bring about rewards which even gods may not be able to grant. Her love and regard for her husband have also grown proportionate to her good fortune. Narayanan is totally dependent on her, not knowing where to look even for a change of clothes. Through daily association with her, Kalyani is changed, changed to a surprising extent. Need anything more be said?

Gopalan passed his BA and is now in medical college studying for the MBCM degree. He and his wife have established good mutual understanding. The extent to which Kalyani has advanced in the study of Tamil and English indicates her sharp intelligence. They now have a baby girl who is always with Savithri. The time that is not taken up tending Gopalan's children, Savithri spends in study and in teaching Kalyani, as well as seven or eight little girls. As she lives with her brother, she has no expenses, and uses the income from her share of the property on charity. On Narayanan's recommendation, she pays the school fees for three poor boys from his school. From time to time she donates clothes and money to the poor, in the many hospitals in the city. But any praise of her munificence angers and annoys her. From her face, it looks as though she has no worry in the world.

Pannai Seshier is dead. His wife and her relatives continue to live in his old Ariyur house. Ayyasami vathiar is in charge of the property of the minor. His is a carefree life.

Sangu sold off his share and went away to Bombay, taking Iyengar and Shala with him. He does not communicate with anyone. Some say he is serving a prison sentence for cheating a merchant. There is another rumour that he has converted to Islam because he loved a Muslim woman and he now goes about as Veera Muhammed Sahib. Yet others say that he was murdered by Iyengar and Shala, who are now enjoying his wealth. No one knows the truth.

Readers who have patiently followed our tale so far, may ask why we have stopped at just three years after the recorded events. They may want more up to date information about our friends. But if that is revealed, there may be efforts to find their true identity and our friends would then be troubled by people calling on them and writing letters to them.

There is just one more thing we would like to say. If any of you vow that you will not eat until you have traced the identity of our friends by looking through the Calendar of the Madras University for their names, you might as well throw away the stoves from your kitchen, as there would be no need for cooking any more.

A Note on Padmavati Part Three

In 1924, twenty three years after the two-part novel had appeared, Madhavaih began a sequel – *Padmavati Charithiram Part Three*, as a serial in his own magazine *Panchamritham*. The following year, his sudden death and the closure of the magazine brought it to an abrupt end, after eighteen chapters.

The interval of a quarter century in the writing of the original and the sequel meant a significant change in the focus of the novel. The concern shifts from the problems of young men of rural, agrarian families, exposed to an English education, to those of the emerging urban, professional middle class. The narrative style too is very different, the story unfolding mainly through conversations, with few descriptive passages, authorial interventions or poetic embellishments.

Padmavati and Narayanan share an active social life, but Padmavati's parents are strongly critical of their daughter's interests outside the home and family, and of their son-in-law's rejection of brahminical orthodoxy. They decide to return to their village and Padmavati has to cope with domestic problems. The parents' tirade against the daughter's neglect of her responsibilities, and the description of the experience with a series of cooks, are delightfully contemporary. However, this sequel mainly revolves around Gopalan. His wife Kalyani dies and he is urged by his relatives to remarry. But he is in love with a young Indian Christian woman, whose father insists on conversion as a precondition to marriage. Narayanan and Padmavati are sympathetic and supportive of Gopalan in his dilemma. Gopalan is distraught, but begins to show an inclination to take the plunge. Opposition arises from an unexpected quarter. Gopalan's children, who have overheard references to their father's romance, are distressed, and decide to write and tell him of their feelings. This is the point at which the story stops.

Chronology

1872:   Madhaviah is born at Perunkulam in Tirunelveli district, on August 16.

1887:   He passed the Matriculation examination after early schooling in Tirunelveli.

1887:   He married Meenakshi, eleven years old, at Narasinganallur near Tirunelveli. Later he joined the Madras Christian College and did his FA and BA.

1892:   After passing the Bachelor of Arts examination with a high rank, he worked as a Lecturer in the Madras Christian College. He also took up studying for his Master of Arts degree along with his job. His first English poem, "To my Alma Mater" appeared in the Madras Christian College Magazine. Seventeen pieces consisting of poems and articles and five essays which made up *Thillai Govindan*'s *Miscellany* appeared in that magazine between 1892 and 1910. Sometime during 1892, he appeared for and easily cleared the competitive examination of the Salt and Abkari Department and entered that service. During his career, he was posted to various places in Andhra Pradesh, Karnataka, Kerala, Orissa and Tamil Nadu including: Thachanallur, Morekulam (near Ramanathapuram), Markapur, Palghat, Hospet, Surla, Kattumavadi, Cheyyar, Tarangampadi, Thanjavur and Ganjam.

He also began writing around this time. He began a novel, *Savithri Charithiram* in the very first issue of the new Tamil journal, *Viveka Chintamani*. This was the first Tamil novel after Vedanayam Pillai's *Pratapa Mudaliar Charithiram* published in 1879. However, it was discontinued after four or five instalments.

1903:   *Savithri Charithiram* revised, completed and published as *Muthumeenakshi*. Also published *Vijayamartandam, Thillai Govindan*..

1914: In a poetry competition for Tamil verses on patriotic themes in simple style, he won the first prize for his "Indhia Kummi." The highpoint of this win was that the noted nationalist poet Subrahmanya Bharathi had also participated in this contest.

1917: Joined like-minded friends to start "Thamizhar Kalai Sangam" with the object of promoting Tamil studies.

1920: Posting in Madras. Rented a house at 79, Bells Road, Triplicane. Contributed several articles to the journal *Thamizhar Nesan*.

1922: Opted for premature retirement, commuted his pension and built a house in Edward Elliots Road , Mylapore. Started his own printing press in an adjoining building in the same compound.

1925: Started a journal *Panchamritham* in April. Died on October 22, at the Senate House, Madras, after a speech advocating the introduction of Tamil as a compulsory subject in the Degree course. The last issue of *Panchamritham* brought out in November, included an elegy on him by Francis Kingsbury.

BIBLIOGRAPHY

In Tamil
Novels

1.	*Padmavati Charithiram*	1898
2.	*Muthumeenakshi*	1903
	(Translated into English by one of his daughters)	
3.	*Vijayamartandam*	1903

Short Stories

1.	*Kusikar Kutti Kathaigal* – 2 parts	1924
	Translated by the author from his English version	

Plays

1.	*Udhayalan* – A free translation or transcreation of *Othello*	1903
2.	*Thirumalai Sethupathi*	1910
3.	*Barrister Panchanatham*	1924
4.	*Manimekalai Thuravu*	1918
5.	*Rajamartandam*	1919

Poetry and Verse

1.	*Podhu Dharma Sangeetha Manjari*	1914
2.	*Pudhumadhiri Kalyanappattu*	1923
3.	*Indhia Desiya Geethangal*	1925

Prose Works, including children's literature

1.	*Aasara Seerthirutham*	1916
2.	*Siddharthan*	1918
3.	*Bala Vinodha Kathaigal*	1923
4.	*Bala Ramayanam*	1924
5.	*Kural Naanuru* in association with Francis Kingsbury, 400 selections from *Thirukkural*, annotated	1924
6.	*Dakshina Charithra Veerarhal*	1925
7.	*Dalavai Mudaliar Kudumba Varalaru*	1924
	Translated by the author from his English version	

8. In addition to these articles, poems, serialized novels, commentary, et cetera that appeared in his magazine, *Panchamritham*, in 1924 and 1925.

In English
Novels

1.	*Thillai Govindan*	1903
2.	*Thillai Govindan* Republished in England by Fisher Unwin, Translated into Tamil by V Narayanan	1916
3.	*Satyananda* Translated into Tamil by Sarojini Packiamuthu (1979)	1909
4.	*The Story of the Ramayana*	1914
5.	*Clarinda* Translated into Tamil by Sarojini Packiamuthu (1976)	1915
6.	*Lieutenant Panju*	1915
7.	*Markandeya*	1922
8.	*Nanda*	1923
9.	*Manimekalai*	1923

Short stories

1. *Kusika's Short Stories* – Two volumes 1916 and in 1923-24, under the pen name "Narada" and the general heading "Stories from Indian Life," A Madhaviah published twenty three short stories in The Hindu, Madras.

Poetry and other prose works

1.	*Poems* (A volume of 20 poems, long and short)	1903
2.	*Dox vs Dox poems*	1903
3.	*Thillai Govindan's Miscellany*, reprinted from the Madras Christian College Magazine	1907
4.	*The Ballad of the Penniless Bride* (A little booklet)	1915
5.	*Dalavai Mudaliar*	1924

Other than this A Madhaviah published, between 1892 and 1910, sixteen articles/poems in the Madras Christian College Magazine.

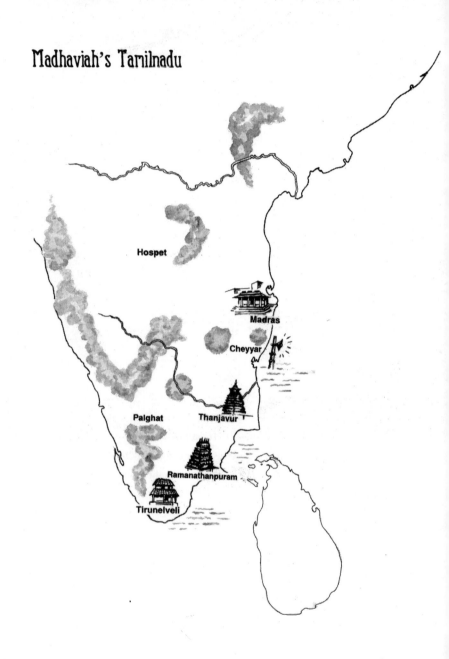

Madhaviah's Tamilnadu

Hospet

Madras

Cheyyar

Palghat

Thanjavur

Ramanathanpuram

Tirunelveli

MEENAKSHI TYAGARAJAN, daughter of Meenambal, the eldest of Madhaviah's children, studied in Bangalore and Madras and did her doctorate in Economics from the United States. She worked in economic research and taught at the Annamalai University. Later she joined the Economic Department of the Reserve Bank of India and retired as Adviser. Since her retirement in 1985, she has been living in Chennai, cultivating her interest in literature and Carnatic music.

A MADHAVAN, son of Anantanarayanan, the eldest son of Madhaviah, completed his post graduation in Madras and joined the Indian Foreign Service. He served in several countries as a diplomat – the last two postings being ambassador to Japan and Germany. After retirement, he was Director, India International Centre, New Delhi, for three years. Since 1995 he is settled in Mysore pursuing his lifelong interest in literature, history and the arts.

M KRISHNAN, youngest son of Madhaviah, was passionately interested in the study of nature and wildlife and his skills as a writer, photographer and artist made him one of India's pioneering naturalists campaigning for the conservation of the country's natural heritage. In 1950, he began a fortnightly column, "Country Notebook," in the *Sunday Statesman*, which continued without a break for forty six years until his death. His writings spanned a wide variety of subjects including art, literature and music. One of the first recipients of the Jawaharlal Nehru Fellowship, he was also honoured with the Padma Shri and the Global Five Hundred Roll of Honour. His books include *Jungle and Backyard*, *Indian Elephant*, *India's Wildlife* and *Nights and Days*. A selection of his writings, *Nature's Spokesman*, was published posthumously in 2000.

MUKTA VENKATESH (maiden name Muthulakshmi), the fourth of Madhaviah's daughters was an Honours student at Queen Mary's College, Madras when she got married. From childhood she was interested in art, particularly painting. She has painted many watercolour flower studies and landscapes and her works have been displayed in exhibitions. Completing her hundredth year in May 2002, she continues to paint and enjoys books on English literature.

ABOUT KATHA

Katha, a registered nonprofit organization set up in September 1989, works in the areas of education, publishing and community development and endeavours to spread the joy of reading, knowing and living amongst adults and children. Our main objective is **to enhance the pleasures of reading for children and adults**, for experienced readers as well as for those who are just beginning to read. Our attempt is also to stimulate an interest in lifelong learning that will help the child grow into a confident, self-reliant, responsible and responsive adult, as also to help break down gender, cultural and social stereotypes, encourage and foster excellence, applaud quality literature and translations in and between the various Indian languages and work towards community revitalization and economic resurgence. The two wings of Katha are **Katha Vilasam** and **Kalpavriksham**

KATHA VILASAM, the Story Research and Resource Centre, was set up to foster and applaud quality Indian literature and take these to a wider audience through quality translations and related activities like **Katha Books, Academic Publishing**, the **Katha Awards** for fiction, translation and editing, **Kathakaar** – the Centre for Children's Literature, **Katha Barani** – the Translation Resource Centre, the **Katha Translation Exchange Programme, Translation Contests. Kanchi** – the Katha National Institute of Translation promotes translation through **Katha Academic Centres** in various Indian universities, **Faculty Enhancement programmes** through Workshops, seminars and discussions, **Sishya** – Katha Clubs in colleges, **Storytellers Unlimited** – the art and craft of storytelling and **KathaRasa** – performances, art fusion and other events at the Katha Centre.

KALPAVRIKSHAM, the Centre for Sustainable Learning, was set up to foster quality education that is relevant and fun for children from nonliterate families, and to promote community revitalization and economic resurgence work. These goals crystallized in the development of the following areas of activities. **Katha Khazana** which includes **Katha Student Support Centre, Katha Public School, Katha School of Entrepreneurship, KITES** – the Katha Information Technology and eCommerce School, **Iccha Ghar** – **The Intel Computer Clubhouse @ Katha, Hamara Gaon** and **The Mandals** – Maa, Bapu, Balika, Balak and Danadini, **Shakti Khazana** was set up for skills upgradation and income generation activities comprising the Khazana Coop. **Kalpana Vilasam** is the cell for regular research and development of teaching/learning materials, curricula, syllabi, content comprising **Teacher Training, TaQeEd — The teachers Alliance for Quality eEducation. Tamasha's World!** comprises **Tamasha! the Children's magazine,** *Dhammakdhum! www.tamasha.org* and ANU – Animals, Nature and YOU!